Report on
PERINATAL STATISTICS
for 2003

Sheelagh Bonham

Health Policy and Information Division
HIPE & NPRS Unit, ESRI

HIPE: Hospital In-Patient Enquiry

NPRS: National Perinatal Reporting System

December 2006

Acknowledgements

The collection and analysis of national perinatal data is a large undertaking and the compilation of an accurate and comprehensive database on a timely basis is greatly dependent on the commitment and support of those at the forefront of collecting the data. Principal among these are the staff of the maternity hospitals and units as well as the many independent midwives involved in practice. We would like to express our sincere appreciation to all who contribute to the accurate recording and timely notification of statistical information for all births nationally.

Data on just over 61,989 births were analysed for this report. For each of these records additional information, apart from that required to register each birth, had to be collected in each hospital and by each independent midwife. This information was compiled and validated by the National Perinatal Reporting System (NPRS) within the Health Policy & Information Division to create a national database, which has been analysed for the production of this report of perinatal events.

In addition to funding the work of the HIPE & NPRS Unit at the ESRI, the Department of Health and Children continues to provide essential support for the operation and development of the NPRS. We would like to acknowledge, in particular, the advice and assistance provided by Hugh Magee and Ciara O'Shea in the preparation of this report. We are also very grateful to Dr. Michael Robson, Master, National Maternity Hospital, Dublin for his valuable input and comments on an earlier draft of this report.

The production of this publication has been a team effort. I would especially like to acknowledge Kate McMenamin's contribution in data preparation, editing and proofreading. I would also like to thank Brian McCarthy and Shane McDermott for their work on the development of the NPRS software system for data entry and validation. Further thanks are due to Deirdre Murphy, Jacqueline O'Reilly, Aisling Mulligan, Fionnola Kelly and Catherine Glennon who have worked directly on the collection and analysis of the data presented in this report and Professor Miriam Wiley for assistance with finalising the report for publication.

Many thanks to our ESRI colleagues Deirdre Whitaker and Pat Hopkins for the assistance provided in the preparation of this report for printing.

We hope that the production of this report by the ESRI will allow national statistics on perinatal events to be observed over time. This report highlights the richness of the resource offered by high quality, timely and accurate data for research and evaluation of perinatal events, in particular, and health and health care services at the population level.

Sheelagh Bonham
National Perinatal Reporting System Manager, ESRI

Table of Contents

List of Tables

Live Births, Stillbirths, Early Neonatal Deaths and Mortality Rates for Multiple Births
for the year 2003 for the following variables:

Live Births, Stillbirths, Early Neonatal Deaths and Mortality Rates for Singleton Births
for the year 2003 for the following variables:

Live Births, Stillbirths, Early Neonatal Deaths and Mortality Rates for Multiple Births
for the year 2003 for the following variables:

The following Tables are based on Live and Still Singleton Births for the year 2003:

List of Figures

Executive Summary

The principal aim of the National Perinatal Reporting System (NPRS) is the provision of national statistics on perinatal events in Ireland. Since 1999, The Economic and Social Research Institute (ESRI) has been contracted by the Department of Health and Children to oversee the collection, processing, management and reporting of data submitted to the NPRS. In this report, data on pregnancy outcomes, with particular reference to perinatal mortality and important aspects of perinatal care, are presented for 2003. In addition, descriptive social and biological characteristics of mothers giving birth and babies born in 2003 are recorded.

In 2003, 61,989 births were notified to the NPRS, an increase of 1.8 per cent since 2002 and 14.1 per cent since 1999. Of these, 357 were stillbirths giving a stillbirth rate of 5.8 per 1,000 live and still births in 2003. The stillbirth rate was slightly lower in previous years: 5.6 per 1,000 live and still births in 2002 and 5.3 per 1,000 live and still births in 1999. There were 177 early neonatal deaths resulting in an early neonatal death rate of 2.9 per 1,000 live births in 2003. This rate represents an increase of 0.1 per 1,000 live births from 2002 (early neonatal death rate of 2.8 per 1,000 live births), but was unchanged from the rate reported in 1999. The perinatal mortality rate was 8.6 per 1,000 live and still births in 2003, an increase of 0.2 per 1,000 from 2002 (perinatal mortality rate of 8.4 per 1,000 live and still births). The 2003 perinatal mortality rate was also higher than that reported in 1999 (8.2 per 1,000 live and still births).

The average birthweight of babies born in 2003 was estimated at 3,471grams, virtually no change from 2002. Average gestational age at delivery in 2003 of 39.4 weeks remained quite constant since 1999. Low birthweight babies (weighing less than 2,500grams) accounted for 5.1 per cent of all births in 2003, a slight increase from 5.0 per cent in 1999. The twinning rate for 2003 was 14.3 per 1,000 maternities, and comprised 873 twin births and 26 triplet births.

In 2003, single mothers accounted for 30 per cent of all women giving birth, which has remained relatively stable over the 5-year period since 1999. Mother's average age increased slightly from 30.1 years in 1999 to 30.6 years in 2003. There has also been a small increase in the average age of single mothers, which was just under 25 years in 1999 and 26 years in 2003. The average maternal parity fell slightly from 1.10 previous births in 1999 to 1.05 in 2003. The trend in the breastfeeding rate continues to be upward at 41.3 per cent in 2003, compared with 41.1 per cent in 2002.

Compared to previous years, 2003 saw a decrease in the number of home births attended by independent domiciliary midwives, (288 in 2002 compared to 236 in 2003 - a decrease of 18.1 per cent in 2003 relative to the previous year). Over the period 1999 to 2003 the number of births attended by independent domiciliary midwives births fell by 4.1 per cent (from 246 in 1999 to 236 in 2003).

Delivery by caesarean section was estimated at 24.2 per cent of all live births in 2003, compared with 22.4 per cent in 2002 and 20.4 per cent in 1999. In 2003, 23.1 per cent of singleton births were delivered by caesarean section, an increase of 1.5 percentage points from 2002. The 2003 caesarean section rate for singleton births also exceeded that reported in 1999 (19.7 per cent of all live singleton births). The percentage of multiple births delivered by caesarean section in 2003 was 58.3 per cent, an increase of 8.8 percentage points from 2002 and over 10 percentage points higher than that reported in 1999. The proportion of all births delivered by caesarean section increased by 3.7 percentage points relative to that estimated for 1999. The increase in the caesarean section rate between 1999 and 2003 was greater for multiple births compared to singleton births.

Average lengths of stay for both mother and infant continued to decline in 2003. Infant's length of stay decreased from an average of 4.3 days in 1999 to 3.8 days in 2003, while mother's average total length of stay fell from 4.7 days in 1999 to 4.0 days in 2003.

The proportion of early neonatal deaths undergoing post-mortem examinations fell from 73.8 per cent in 1992 to a low of 33.6 per cent in 2001. This estimate increased to 42.1 per cent in 2002 but fell to 41.7 per cent in 2003.

Section 1
Introduction

Aims

This report of the National Perinatal Reporting System (NPRS) has as its principal aim the provision of national statistics on perinatal events for the year 2003. More specifically, the report aims to describe the fundamental social and biological characteristics of mothers and their babies, to report on pregnancy outcomes with particular reference to perinatal mortality, and to highlight important aspects of perinatal care. Although great strides have been made in reducing infant and perinatal mortality during the past twenty years, the perinatal period continues to be a time of relatively high mortality. Set in this context, the importance of monitoring variables related to perinatal health becomes evident.

This report presents what might be considered a minimum national data set and is intended to serve as a foundation for the development of basic time series analyses and to allow for the possible addition of further variables and more extensive analysis in future years. In mid-2003 the birth notification form was revised to facilitate a number of new fields that were required by the General Register Office (part 1) for birth registrations. These changes have resulted in the collection of two new variables, nationality and country of residence for both the mother and father, by the NPRS. These variables will be reported in the national statistics from 2004. It is hoped that the publication of the data reported to the NPRS will stimulate a wider interest in research in the area of perinatal epidemiology and promote a general recognition of the importance of having an accurate and complete perinatal reporting system. For background information on the development of the perinatal reporting system please see previous reports (HIPE & NPRS Unit, Report on Perinatal Statistics for 2002, Economic and Social Research Institute, 2005).

Data Collection and Processing

Births are registered and notified on a standard four-part form (see Appendix B). The top copy of the form is sent by the hospital to the Registrar of Births and serves as the official document of registration. This copy is subsequently forwarded to the Central Statistics Office for use in the production of quarterly and annual reports on vital statistics. The second part of the form containing additional information on the health of the mother and the infant and on the care received goes to the Director of Community Care and Medical Officer of Health in the mother's area of residence. It serves the dual purpose of notifying the local medical and nursing services that have responsibility for the postnatal care of the mother and child and of providing the basis for health records used by the health boards. The third part of the form has all identifying information deleted and is sent to the NPRS Unit at The Economic and Social Research Institute (ESRI). The fourth and final copy is retained by the hospital. For domiciliary births, the same four-part form is used and the first three parts are processed as with hospital births while Part 4 is retained by the midwife. Figure 1.1 provides a diagrammatic representation of the information system.   All the tables in the present report are based on data contained in the third copy of the standard form.

Figure 1.1
National Perinatal Reporting System, Diagrammatic View

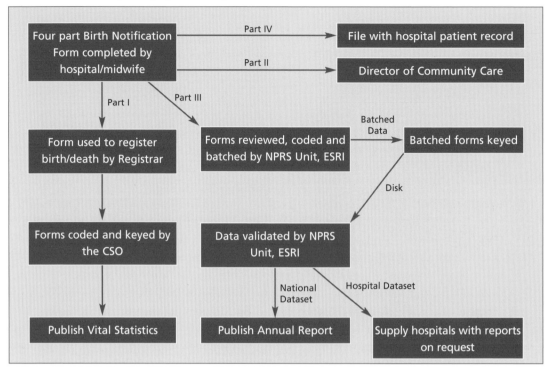

The data collected by the National Perinatal Reporting System can be logically grouped into demographic, clinical and administrative data. The data collected by the NPRS for 2003 include:

- Demographic Data
  Date of infant's birth; sex of infant; multiple birth indicator;
  Date of father's birth; father's county of residence; father's occupation;
  Date of mother's birth; mother's county of residence; mother's occupation;
  Marital status of mother and date of present marriage.

- Clinical Data
  Infant's birthweight and period of gestation; mother's obstetric history;
  Autopsy indicator; whether stillbirth occurred before or during labour;
  Main cause of death and one secondary cause of death for infant;
  Maternal immunity to rubella; method of delivery;
  Infant's BCG vaccination;
  Main maternal disease or condition and one secondary maternal disease or condition affecting the infant or foetus;
  Main disease or congenital malformation and one secondary disease or congenital malformation affecting the infant or foetus.

- Administrative Data
  Hospital number; case number (unique to hospital of birth);
  Type of birth indicator; place of birth;
  Date of last birth (live or still);
  Type of death indicator; place of death;
  Type of antenatal care received; date of first visit to doctor and hospital during pregnancy;
  Type of feeding; pre-booked admission indicator; dates of mother's admission and discharge; date of infant's discharge;
  Infant transfer indicator; hospital number for hospital to which infant was transferred.

Occupations are coded according to the Central Statistics Office system of socio-economic group classification (see Appendix C, page 101). Diseases and cause of death are coded using the ninth revision of the International Classification of Diseases (ICD) and according to the guidelines set out by the World Health Organisation (see Appendix D, page 103). On completion of data entry, the NPRS Unit in The Health Policy and Information Division at the ESRI undertakes checks for data coverage and validation.

Format and Contents

This report presents a set of national tabulations for perinatal events for 2003 indicating frequencies, stillbirth rates, early neonatal death rates, and perinatal mortality rates set out for a number of the most important social, biological and health care variables. The data are presented in four main sections covering selected trends, general characteristics, perinatal care and perinatal outcomes. The definitions for parameters reported in these sections are contained in Appendix A. Section 2 (Selected Trends) documents significant trends in the principal variables for the years 1991-1993 and 1999-2003. Section 3 contains tables relating to the following variables: maternal age; parity; marital status; socio-economic group of mother; socio-economic group of father; distribution of previous stillbirths; birthweight (by sex); twinning rate; gestational age; interval since last birth and month of birth.

Section 4 deals with variables which fall more naturally into the category of use of health care facilities and type of antenatal care received and deals with the following distributions: type of antenatal care received; length of mother's antenatal stay; length of mother's postnatal stay; mother's immunity to rubella; method of delivery; whether hospital admission was booked or not; type of feeding; transfer of infants between hospitals and classification of outcome according to size of maternity unit.

In Section 5, causes of perinatal deaths and other factors closely related to the outcome of pregnancy are considered. In this section tables are presented on the following variables: numbers of antepartum and intrapartum stillbirths by birthweight groups; numbers and rates for cause of death and cause of death by birthweight; age at death for early neonatal deaths; numbers and percentages of stillbirths and early neonatal deaths undergoing post-mortem examinations and the length of infant's stay in hospital. It should be noted that Sections 3, 4 and 5 are each divided into two parts: Part 1 relates to singleton births and Part 2 relates to multiple births.

Completeness and Reliability

Coverage

The National Perinatal Reporting System covers all live births and stillbirths occurring in Ireland. However, there are differences in the vital statistics published by the Central Statistics Office and the data presented in this report. The reasons for this are outlined below.

Missing Values

No attempt has been made to assign values to missing data, and they are included as a separate category in each table. Each year the proportion of cases with the value 'not stated' continues to decline. This is a positive outcome arising from continued effort on the part of the NPRS staff, hospital administrators and independent midwives to reduce the number of missing values for all variables collected in the data set. This improves the completeness of the reported data, which is a key objective for the NPRS.

Two new variables, nationality and country of residence for both the mother and father, were introduced in May 2003. These variables will be reported in the national statistics from 2004 onwards. Father's date of birth and mother's occupation were included for the first time in the report for 1999. For 2003, father's date of birth is missing for 11.0 per cent of births where mother's marital status is married.[1] Missing values for mother's occupation remains very low as just 1.6 per cent of births in 2003 were missing this information.

The majority of variables are virtually complete in the 2003 dataset with 'gestational age at delivery' and 'infant's birthweight' missing for only 14 records. 'Method of delivery' was missing for 9 records while 'infant's feeding' has been recorded as 'not stated' for 20 births. Information on hospital length of stay has also improved with mother's antenatal and postnatal lengths of stay missing for just 10 and 17 records respectively. Infant's length of stay is missing for less than 1 per cent of records.

Notwithstanding improvements in the completeness of returns, the elimination of 'missing values' for all variables continues to be an important objective for the development of the NPRS.

Delivery of Antenatal Care

Changing models of antenatal care are being experienced by mothers in Ireland and it is intended that the data collected by the National Perinatal Reporting System should reflect these changes. The data collected with regard to 'Mother's Health' is intended to describe the mother's first contact with the health services. The data currently collected in this section include the following:

- Type of antenatal care this pregnancy (Hospital/Obstetrician=1, G.P. only=2, Combined=3, None=4, Midwife Only=5).
- Date of first visit to doctor.
- Date of first visit to hospital.

Where 'antenatal care this pregnancy' is indicated as 'combined care', it is expected that the dates of first visit to each health professional is recorded. While over 75 per cent of all births in 2003 were recorded as receiving combined antenatal care, over 40 per cent of these births recorded 'date of first visit to doctor' as 'not known'. The absence of this data regrettably means that the presentation of the timing of first contact with health professionals within this category is somewhat unbalanced.

---

[1] It should be noted that where a mother's marital status is single, widowed, separated or divorced the General Register Office (GRO) does not require father's details to register the birth, and as such this information is generally not provided.

The proportion of mother's attending antenatal care during the first 12 weeks is, therefore, estimated at around 45 per cent of all births, which is low by European standards.

A review of data reported for 'Gestational Age at First Visit to Doctor or Hospital During Pregnancy' was conducted in 2006 and a revised algorithm was used to estimate this indicator for 2003. These data are presented in Appendix I of this report and include revised tables from 1999-2003 data.

Area of Residence

In the interests of safeguarding patient confidentiality, the copy of the notification form received by the NPRS unit at the ESRI does not contain the mother's full address but only the county designation (see Appendix E). As we have no way of validating this information, mother's area of residence has been analysed at health board level in this report.

Data Quality

The NPRS seeks to compile an accurate, complete and up-to-date database on perinatal events over a specified time period. A key issue in addressing the quality of data collected by the NPRS are differences arising between the vital statistics tables compiled by the CSO and the NPRS data. Differences in data reported by these two systems for perinatal events may arise for a variety of reasons. One reason for differences is that information is not always obtained from the same sources. This is particularly evident in the data for cause of death as the CSO and the NPRS have to use different sources for the compilation of these data. The CSO does not obtain information on maternal diseases or conditions affecting the foetus or infant while the NPRS does not have access to coroner's certificates relating to neonatal deaths. The CSO also uses a separate notification form (Form 103) for collecting information on late foetal deaths.

Different data sources are also a factor in explaining why there are differences in the rate of stillbirth reported by the CSO and the NPRS. In 1995, stillbirths were registered in Ireland for the first time under the Stillbirths Registration Act, 1994. The CSO collect these data using Part 1 of the birth notification form sent to the General Register Office (GRO), while the NPRS collect them using Part 3 of the birth notification form. The CSO defines a stillbirth as weighing at or over 500grams and/or at a gestational age of 24 weeks or more. From 1995 onwards, this definition applies to a late foetal death. In accordance with the World Health Organisation's (WHO) definition of a stillbirth, the NPRS includes all late foetal deaths weighing at least 500grams, irrespective of gestational age. In 2003, the NPRS recorded a higher number of stillbirths than the CSO. Applying the CSO's definition of a stillbirth, the number of stillbirths recorded by the NPRS would be estimated at 386 stillbirths. The CSO, however, reports 345 stillbirths indicating that in 2003 a number of stillbirths were notified to NPRS but not registered to the GRO. When we apply the WHO definition of a stillbirth to the data collected by the NPRS, the number of stillbirths recorded by the NPRS is estimated at 357. In accordance with WHO guidelines, only these 357 stillbirths are included in the NPRS dataset for this report. Differences in the definitions of stillbirth used by the CSO and the WHO is, therefore, an important factor in understanding differences in the stillbirth numbers and rates and the perinatal mortality rate reported by the CSO and the NPRS.

The gap between the twinning rate calculated by the CSO and the ESRI is very narrow. For 2003 the CSO report a twinning rate of 14.8 per 1,000 maternities and the NPRS report a twinning rate of 14.3 per 1,000 maternities. The NPRS dataset excludes all births where weight is < 500 grams. In the case of a multiple birth where one or more births from the set weighs <500 grams, the birth/s weighing < 500 grams are removed from the national dataset. Any birth/s weighing >500 grams in the multiple birth set are retained in the national dataset as a multiple birth/s. To clarify using an example: a set of twins are born, twin 1 weighs < 500 grams, twin 2 weighs > 500 grams, twin 1 is removed from the national dataset and twin 2 remains in the national dataset and is recorded as the second twin of a multiple birth. This may result in incomplete sets of multiple births in the national dataset and a lower number of multiple births recorded for reporting purposes (see also Table 3.14). There is a single field on the birth notification form that identifies a multiple birth. If these data were not recorded then the NPRS has no way of identifying multiple births. It would be assumed, however, that the additional personal identification data available to the CSO ensures a more comprehensive estimate of the number of multiple births.

Finally, differences in coding procedures can be reflected in the published statistics. The International Classification of Disease (ICD) coding procedures are recognised as being particularly difficult and subjective in the area of causes of perinatal mortality and the current separate coding arrangements between the CSO and the NPRS can, therefore, lead to significant discrepancies.

Ideally, the data sources and coding for reporting on perinatal events should be harmonised between the CSO and NPRS. Currently representatives of both systems, together with the Department of Health and Children are in the process of putting procedures in place towards the achievement of this objective. The computerisation of the birth registration system represents an important step in this process, as this will eliminate the duplication of paperwork, coding and validation procedures. The General Register Office (GRO) began its national roll-out for the computerisation of birth registration in September 2003. This covers the registration information collected on the top copy of the birth notification form and future phases of the computerisation programme are intended to include all statistical data.

Pending the completion of the full scale programme of computerisation, there are discussions underway between the CSO and the NPRS to put in place a system of downloading the computerised information that is available and linking it electronically with the statistical data captured in Part 3 of the form. While this is envisaged as an interim measure, we would expect that it would assist in ensuring the correct identification of all births and, reduce duplication of effort in keying registered data thereby improving data quality. Because the data for Part 3 of the form still has to be keyed centrally, the HIPE & NPRS Unit at the Health Policy and Information Division at the ESRI have developed an in-house data entry system whereby notifications of births from January 1st 2004 are coded and entered directly onto the NPRS as they are received. This system validates the information received on each form at the point of data entry.

A parallel development aimed at improving the timeliness of data reporting and data quality are initiatives aimed at the electronic transfer of data directly from hospitals. Currently data in electronic format are being received by the NPRS from one major Dublin hospital and it is hoped to expand this development to other hospitals with similar systems capability. Notwithstanding these advancements in the computerisation of data collection and validation, we continue to rely on midwives and hospital staff to provide accurate and up-to-date data to the NPRS. The new instruction manual to facilitate completion of BNF01/2003 issued in May 2003 details the requirements for completion of each field and is intended as an additional aid to personnel completing the returns. The continued development of computerised registration and notification and electronic data transfer are, however, an essential prerequisite to the achievement of the NPRS goal of delivering optimum data quality, timeliness and comprehensive coverage.

General Trends and International Comparisons[2]

Perinatal Mortality

Recent decades have witnessed a substantial decline in infant, neonatal and perinatal mortality in Ireland. Figure 1.2 shows the perinatal mortality rate in Ireland from 1983-2003. These rates are based on the national statistics compiled by the CSO. Between 1965 and 1980 the perinatal mortality rate fell by more than half from 30 deaths per 1,000 live births and stillbirths to 14.8 per 1,000 live births and stillbirths. From 1981 until 1984 the rate remained stable at around 13.5 per 1,000 live births and stillbirths, but resumed its decline to 10.4 per 1,000 live births and stillbirths in 1987 before rising slightly to 11.3 per 1,000 live births and stillbirths in 1988. From 1989 the rate declined relatively steadily from 10.3 per 1,000 live births and stillbirths to a low of 7.5 per 1,000 live births and stillbirths in 1999, which was half the 1980 rate.[3] For 2000, the perinatal mortality rate increased marginally to 7.8 per 1,000 live births and stillbirths, resuming its decline once again in 2001 and 2002 to 7.5 and 7.6 per 1,000 live births and stillbirths respectively. The perinatal mortality rate is reported at 7.1 per 1,000 live births and stillbirths for 2003.

Figure 1.2

Perinatal Mortality Rate, Ireland: 1983-2003

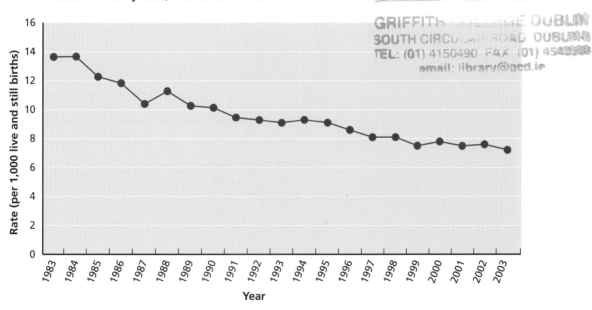

Source: Report on *Vital Statistics, 2003*, Central Statistics Office.

The factors impacting on the level of perinatal mortality are complex and encompass a wide range of environmental and biological variables. Birthweight, parity, mother's age, social status and type of antenatal care as well as many other variables have a bearing on perinatal risk. Data in this report indicate levels of perinatal mortality for the principal variables associated with risk. Ireland's standing in relation to other countries in the European Union (EU) is shown in Figure 1.3. Of the thirteen countries for which data are available from the Eurostat database for 2003, Ireland's perinatal

---

[2] National figures presented in this section are based on official registration data as compiled by the Central Statistics Office. These figures may differ somewhat from numbers and rates appearing in the tables of this report for reasons given in the previous section.
Where the data are available EU comparisons are based on EU membership at time of publication (i.e. twenty-five countries).
[3] In 1995 a revised definition of stillbirths was employed by the CSO. This new definition included stillbirths at or over 500grams or at a gestational age of 24 weeks or more. The data presented here are based on the previous definition of a stillbirth (at or over 28 weeks gestation) to facilitate comparisons over time.

mortality rate is recorded at 7.1 per 1,000, with the United Kingdom and a number of new member states including Hungary, Latvia, Lithuania and Poland showing higher rates. Of the thirteen countries represented here, the Czech Republic records the lowest perinatal mortality rate at 4.3 per 1,000 followed by Portugal with 5.1 per 1,000. When countries are compared it should be remembered that rates are affected by national policies on abortion, by differences in the comprehensiveness and accuracy of registration and notification systems and by differences in definitions employed (for example, for stillbirth).

Figure 1.3
Perinatal Mortality Rate, 2003, for Selected EU Countries

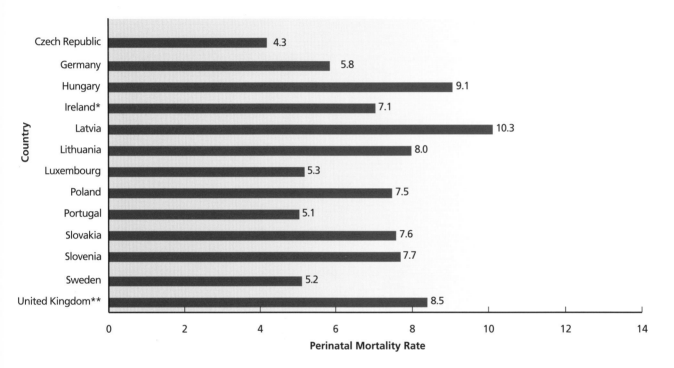

Source: "Population and Social Conditions", Eurostat, Data Navigation Tree, date consulted May 2006.
http://epp.eurostat.cec.eu.int
*National figure compiled by the Central Statistics Office, Report on *Vital Statistics*, 2003.
** *Source:* Office for National Statistics, *Health Statistics Quarterly 24*, Winter 2005.

Birth Rate

Data for births per 1,000 population over the past twenty years illustrate an overall reduction in the crude birth rate of 19 per cent since 1983. From 1983, the birth rate steadily declined from 19.2 per 1,000 population to 14.8 per 1,000 population in 1989. It then rose slightly in 1990 to 15.1 per 1,000 population and then resumed the downward trend to reach an all time low of 13.5 per 1,000 population in 1994. Since 1995 the birth rate has gradually increased to 14.6 per 1,000 population in 1998, and has remained stable up until 2000 at 14.5 per 1,000 population. For 2001 the birth rate increased to 15.0 per 1,000 population and has remained at 15.5 per 1,000 population in 2002 and 2003. This represents a return to the rates experienced in the early 1990s (Figure 1.4).

Figure 1.4
Birth Rate per 1,000 Population, Ireland: 1983-2003

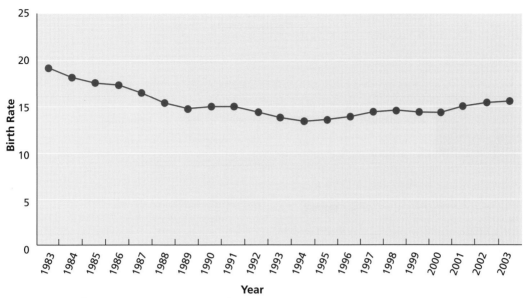

Source; Reports on *Vital Statistics, 1983-2003*, Central Statistics Office.

Figure 1.5 shows trends in birth rates for selected EU countries in the last decade. For the countries reviewed, Ireland has consistently had the highest birth rate over the period. While Ireland's birth rate moved closer to that of other European countries around 1994 and 1995, since 2000 the gap has continued to widen between Ireland and France, the European country closest to Ireland in terms of birth rates. In 2003 Ireland continues to have the highest birth rate of any of the twenty-five EU countries at 15.5 per 1,000 population.

Figure 1.5
Trends in Birth Rates for Selected EU Countries: 1993-2003

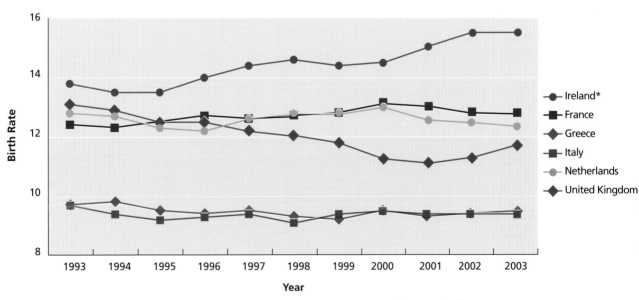

Source: "Population and Social Conditions", Eurostat, Data Navigation Tree, date consulted May 2006.
http://epp.eurostat.cec.eu.int
*National figures. Report on *Vital Statistics, 2003* Central Statistics Office.

Figure 1.6 displays the birth rate per 1,000 population for EU countries in 2003. Apart from Ireland (15.5), the country with the next highest birth rate is France (12.7) followed by the Netherlands (12.3) and Denmark (12.0). In 2003 Germany (8.6) and Slovenia (8.7) had the lowest birth rate followed by Lithuania (8.9) and Latvia (9.0).

Figure 1.6
Birth Rate per 1,000 Population for EU Countries: 2003

Country	Birth Rate per 1,000 Population
Austria	9.5
Belgium	10.8
Cyprus	11.2
Czech Republic	9.2
Denmark	12.0
Estonia	9.6
Finland	10.9
France	12.7
Germany	8.6
Greece	9.5
Hungary	9.3
Ireland*	15.5
Italy	9.4
Latvia	9.0
Lithuania	8.9
Luxembourg	11.8
Malta	10.1
Netherlands	12.3
Poland	9.2
Portugal	10.8
Slovakia	9.6
Slovenia	8.7
Spain	10.5
Sweden	11.1
United Kingdom	11.7

Source: "Population and Social Conditions", Eurostat, Data Navigation Tree, date consulted May 2006.
http://epp.eurostat.cec.eu.int
*National figures. Report on *Vital Statistics, 2003*, Central Statistics Office.

It should be noted that the crude birth rate could rise or fall depending on the numbers of women in the age cohorts from 15-49 years old. Changes in the crude birth rate often mask underlying trends in fertility. The next section is therefore concerned with changes in fertility over time.

Fertility

Figure 1.7 shows the trend in the Total Period Fertility Rate (TPFR) in Ireland over the past twenty years. The TPFR for a given year indicates the number of children a woman could expect to have if the age specific fertility rates for that year applied throughout her fertile years. The Irish TPFR has declined from an average of 2.76 in 1983 to 1.98 in 2003, representing a 28 per cent rate of decrease over 20 years. By 1994 and 1995 the Irish TPFR reached a low of 1.85 but increased again during the latter half of the 1990s. The rise in the crude birth rate over this period was largely accounted for by the increasing numbers of women in the childbearing age groups. As in all twenty-five EU countries currently, the TPFR for Ireland remains below the level required for the long-term replacement of the population (TPFR of 2.1) in the absence of any net inward migration. While Ireland has experienced a fairly rapid fall in TPFR over the past twenty years, the TPFR has been increasing consistently since 2001 and is returning to those rates experienced in Ireland in the early 1990s. Figure 1.8 shows that for 2003 Ireland continues to have the highest TPFR in the EU (1.98) followed by France (1.89 TPFR). For 2003 the Czech Republic, Slovakia and Slovenia have the lowest total period fertility rates (1.18 and 1.20 respectively) within the twenty-five EU countries.

Figure 1.7

Total Period Fertility Rates Subdivided by Age Groups, Ireland: 1983-2003

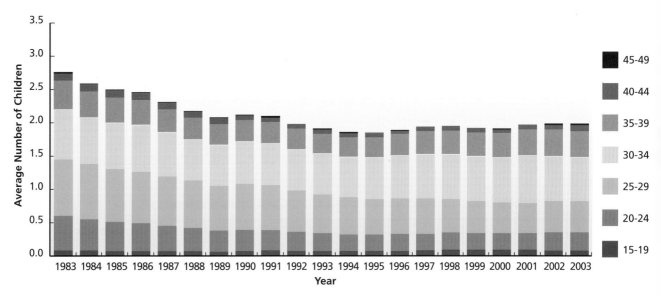

Source: Report on *Vital Statistics, 2003*, Central Statistics Office.

Figure 1.8

Total Period Fertility Rate, 2003, for EU Countries

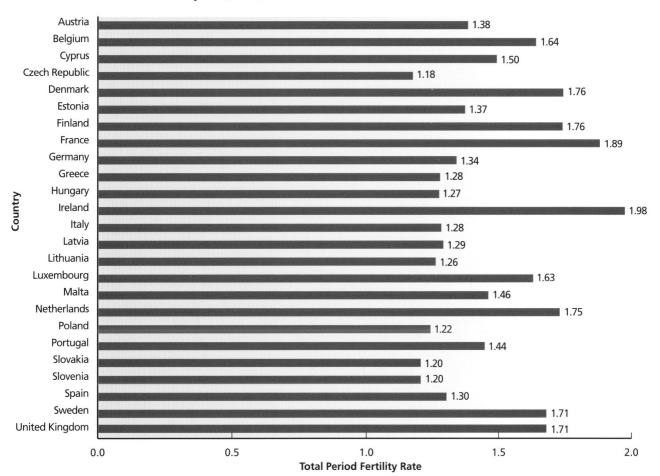

Source: "Population and Social Conditions", Eurostat, Data Navigation Tree, date consulted May 2006.
http://epp.eurostat.cec.eu.int
Note: For comparative purposes all rates (including that for Ireland) for Figure 1.8 are from Eurostat, May 2006.

Section 2
Selected Trends

A general review of the data reported to the NPRS over the period 1991-1993 and 1999-2003 is presented in this section.   Tables 2.1 and 2.2 examine trends in vital and selected statistics for these years. Figures 2.1 to 2.6 present selected data for a number of variables, including single mothers; low birthweight babies; caesarean births; mother's breastfeeding and other aspects of perinatal care. Each of these figures summarise data for 1991-1993 and 1999-2003.

Table 2.1
Vital Events 1991-1993 and 1999-2003

Singleton and Multiple Births, Numbers and Rates (per 1,000) for
Live Births, Stillbirths, Early Neonatal Deaths and Perinatal Deaths

Vital Events		1991		1992		1993		Year 1999		2000		2001		2002		2003	
		Number	Rate	Number	Rate	Number	Rate	Number	Rate	Number	Rate	Number	Rate	Number	Rate	Number	Rate
Live Births:	Singleton	51,242	-	49,686	-	48,030	-	52,556	-	53,429	-	56,115	-	58,752	-	59,837	-
	Multiple	1,200	-	1,182	-	1,001	-	1,463	-	1,429	-	1,807	-	1,770	-	1,795	-
	Total	52,442	-	50,868	-	49,031	-	54,019	-	54,858	-	57,922	-	60,522	-	61,632	-
Stillbirths:	Singleton	284	5.5	285	5.7	272	5.6	274	5.2	288	5.4	307	5.4	319	5.4	327	5.4
	Multiple	18	14.8	16	31.4	11	10.9	14	9.5	20	13.8	32	17.4	24	13.4	30	16.4
	Total	302	5.7	301	5.9	283	5.7	288	5.3	308	5.6	339	5.8	343	5.6	357	5.8
Early Neonatal Deaths	Singleton	195	3.8	173	3.5	131	2.7	130	2.5	153	2.9	136	2.4	149	2.5	156	2.6
	Multiple	24	20.0	19	16.1	16	16.0	27	18.5	23	16.1	24	13.3	21	11.9	21	11.7
	Total	219	4.2	192	3.8	147	3.0	157	2.9	176	3.2	160	2.8	170	2.8	177	2.9
Perinatal Deaths	Singleton	479	9.3	458	9.2	403	8.3	404	7.6	441	8.2	443	7.9	468	7.9	483	8.0
	Multiple	42	34.5	35	29.2	27	26.7	41	27.8	43	29.7	56	30.5	45	25.1	51	27.9
	Total	521	9.9	493	9.6	430	8.7	445	8.2	484	8.8	499	8.6	513	8.4	534	8.6
Adjusted Perinatal Deaths	Singleton	320	6.2	318	6.4	294	6.1	301	5.7	317	5.9	311	5.5	353	6.0	336	5.6
	Multiple	39	32.1	32	26.8	18	17.9	37	25.1	31	21.6	45	24.6	43	24.0	48	26.3
	Total	359	6.8	350	6.9	312	6.3	338	6.2	348	6.3	356	6.1	396	6.5	384	6.2

Table 2.2

Trends in Selected Statistics, 1991-1993 and 1999-2003

Selected Statistics	1991	1992	1993	1999	2000	2001	2002	2003
General Characteristics								
Average Age of Mother in years	29.11	29.18	29.30	30.06	30.18	30.27	30.41	30.58
Average Maternal Parity	1.43	1.37	1.33	1.10	1.09	1.07	1.06	1.05
Single Mothers (%)	15.54	16.50	18.14	29.71	30.09	30.14	30.01	30.20
Average Age of Single Mothers in years	22.36[E]	22.41[E]	22.83[E]	24.74	24.98	25.36	25.72	26.10
Average Number of Previous Stillbirths per 1,000 maternities	17.22	19.82	23.18	14.03	13.06	13.57	12.58	12.61
Average weight in grams - Singleton Births	3,548.02	3,525.01	3,520.02	3,505.35	3,517.36	3,509.36	3,503.73	3,500.64
- Multiple Births	2,653.17	2,549.84	2,535.38	2,467.24	2,509.85	2,470.41	2,489.72	2,487.13
- Total Births	3,527.54	3,502.37	3,499.98	3,477.19	3,491.13	3,476.96	3,474.07	3,471.11
Low birthweight <2500 grams (%)								
- Singleton Births	3.43	3.24	3.39	3.80	3.84	3.84	3.76	3.87
- Multiple Births	38.38	41.38	42.23	47.71	43.35	46.46	44.18	45.07
- Total Births	4.23	4.13	4.18	4.99	4.87	5.17	4.94	5.07
Average Gestational Age at delivery in weeks	39.59	40.23	40.08	39.48	39.46	39.47	39.45	39.44
Average interval since last birth in years	3.68	3.69	3.75	3.82	3.84	3.81	3.85	3.78
Perinatal Care								
Hospital & GP combined antenatal care (%)	58.97	61.97	63.94	72.30	72.39	73.25	74.06	75.85
Mother's average length of stay in days	5.24	5.12	5.15	4.71	4.54	4.38	4.09	3.95
Immunity to Rubella (%)	89.40	89.02	89.36	89.63	87.76	86.84	86.49	87.30
Method of Delivery (%) [1,2] *Singleton Births*								
- Spontaneous	73.64	73.72	72.95	65.35	64.56	64.29	63.27	62.24
- Caesarean	11.30	11.78	12.57	19.69	20.55	21.05	21.61	23.14
- Forceps [3]	9.58	8.30	7.79	4.27	3.78	3.21	3.19	2.89
Multiple Births								
- Spontaneous	39.36	40.78	37.99	32.33	33.73	29.83	33.62	26.30
- Caesarean	30.70	29.69	34.95	47.23	50.31	52.74	49.49	58.33
- Forceps [3]	8.07	6.40	6.48	3.08	2.52	2.71	2.99	1.56
Total Births								
- Spontaneous	72.85	72.96	72.24	64.46	63.76	63.22	62.41	61.20
- Caesarean	11.75	12.19	13.03	20.43	21.33	22.04	22.43	24.17
- Forceps [3]	9.54	8.25	7.77	4.24	3.74	3.20	3.18	2.85
Booked Hospital Admissions (%)	98.94	98.99	98.46	96.49	96.48	98.17	97.58	97.47
Mother's breastfeeding (%)	31.85	33.85	33.89	36.16	38.41	39.13	41.14	41.32
Perinatal Outcomes								
Wigglesworth Classes (Rate) [4]								
- Macerated Stillbirths	2.96	3.48	3.10	3.46	4.04	3.67	4.23	3.84
- Congenital Anomalies	2.88	2.74	2.37	1.94	2.46	2.50	1.87	2.37
- Immaturity	1.44	1.48	1.20	1.39	1.07	1.27	1.23	1.18
- Asphyxia	2.39	1.74	1.91	1.93	1.38	1.49	1.43	1.52
- Specific Conditions	0.38	0.47	0.43	0.49	0.51	0.63	0.64	0.53
- Total	10.05	9.91	9.00	9.11	9.45	9.57	9.40	9.43
Infant's average length of stay in days								
- Singleton Births	4.41	4.44	4.52	4.17	4.08	3.89	3.68	3.62
- Multiple Births	7.83	9.56	11.27	10.68	10.73	11.45	10.16	10.09
- Total Births	4.47	4.54	4.59	4.34	4.25	4.12	3.87	3.80
Post-mortems for Early Neonatal Deaths (%)	66.12	73.78	66.67	44.37	39.41	33.55	42.07	41.72

[1] See Tables 4.4 and 4.13 for data on all Methods of Delivery.
[2] These figures were not based on total maternities but on total births, to give a more accurate picture as each infant in a multiple pregnancy can have a different method of delivery.
[3] Excludes breech deliveries.
[4] See Appendix G for details of method.

E= Estimate. Weighted averages from data in Appendix E, Table 3, Reports on *Perinatal Statistics, 1991-1993*, Department of Health.

Note: These selected statistics are set out according to the order in which they appear in subsequent sections of this report. Further details for each statistic, including mortality rates, are given in these sections. Statistics relating to maternal characteristics are based on total maternities. Missing values are not included in the calculation of percentages.

Figure 2.1

Percentage of Births to Single Mothers, 1991-1993 and 1999-2003

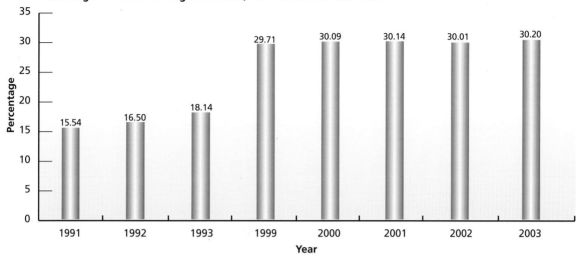

Figure 2.2

Percentage of Births to Single Mothers by Age of Mother, Singleton Births, 1991-1993 and 1999-2003

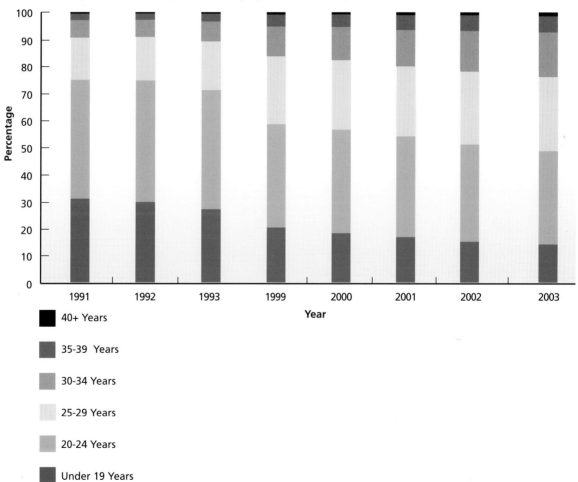

Source: Reports on *Perinatal Statistics, 1991-1993*, Department of Health. Appendix E, Table 3.
Reports on *Perinatal Statistics for 1999-2002*, The Economic & Social Research Institute. Appendix E, Tables E3.
Note: See Appendix F, Table F3 for data on 2003.

Figure 2.3
Percentage of Low Birthweight Babies, 1991-1993 and 1999-2003

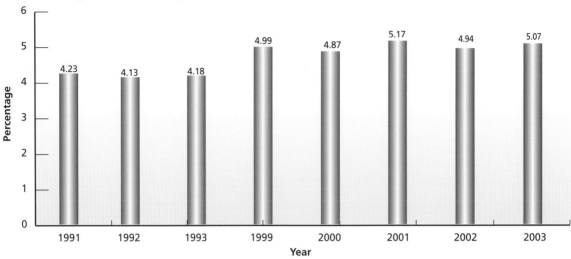

Figure 2.4
Average Length of Stay in Days for Mothers and Infants, 1991-1993 and 1999-2003

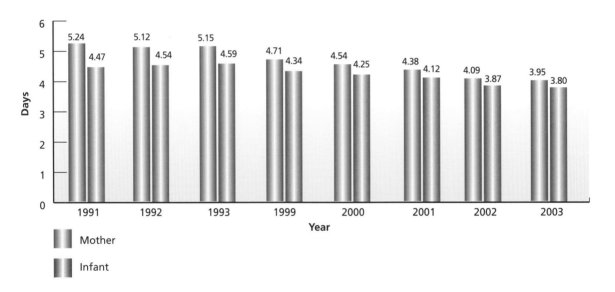

Figure 2.5

Caesarean Births as a Percentage of Total Births, 1991-1993 and 1999-2003

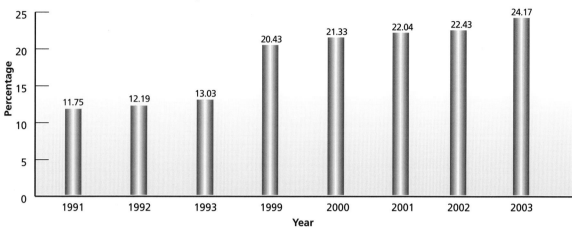

Figure 2.6

Percentage of Mother's Breastfeeding, 1991-1993 and 1999-2003

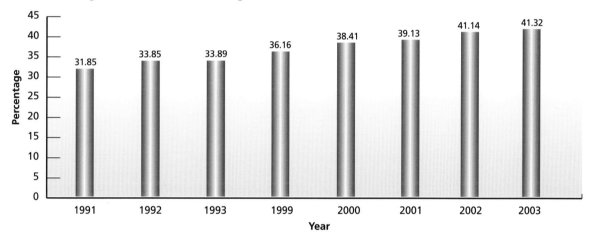

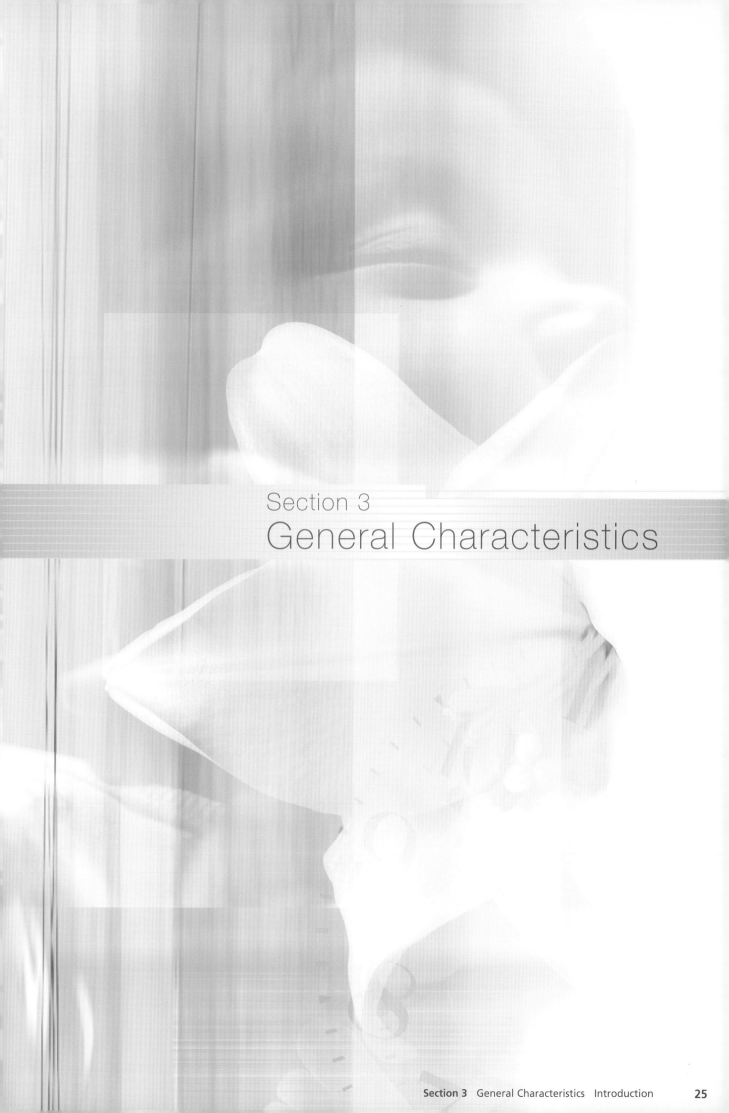

Section 3
General Characteristics

This section presents a more detailed analysis of data reported to the NPRS for 2003. Part 1 reports on singleton births and Part 2 on multiple births. The following tables outline data for live births, stillbirths and early neonatal deaths, together with their corresponding rates. The perinatal mortality rate and adjusted perinatal mortality rate are also outlined in each table. Tables and figures are presented in some detail for a number of variables, including mother's age; marital status; father and mother's occupation; birthweight and mother's health board of residence.

Section 3
General Characteristics

Part 1 Singleton Births

Section 3 General Characteristics
Part 1 Singleton Births

Table 3.1
Age of Mother

Live Births, Stillbirths, Early Neonatal Deaths and Mortality Rates, 2003

Singleton Births

Age of Mother	Live Births	Per Cent (%) Live Births	Stillbirths	Stillbirth Rate	Early Neonatal Deaths	Early Neonatal Rate	Perinatal Mortality Rate	Adjusted PMR*
Under 15 Years	14	0.0	1	66.7	0	0.0	66.7	66.7
15-19 Years	2,799	4.7	23	8.2	12	4.3	12.4	9.2
20-24 Years	8,311	13.9	50	6.0	24	2.9	8.9	7.2
25-29 Years	14,369	24.0	58	4.0	32	2.2	6.2	4.2
30-34 Years	20,449	34.2	106	5.2	53	2.6	7.7	5.6
35-39 Years	11,609	19.4	58	5.0	25	2.2	7.1	4.2
40-44 Years	2,171	3.6	20	9.1	10	4.6	13.7	8.3
45 Years & over	65	0.1	1	15.2	0	0.0	15.2	0.0
Not Stated	50	0.1	10	166.7	0	0.0	166.7	137.9
Total	**59,837**	**100.0**	**327**	**5.4**	**156**	**2.6**	**8.0**	**5.6**

*In this and subsequent tables, 'Adjusted PMR' gives a recalculated perinatal mortality rate which excludes all deaths due to congenital anomalies.

Table 3.2
Maternal Parity

Live Births, Stillbirths, Early Neonatal Deaths and Mortality Rates, 2003

Singleton Births

Maternal Parity	Live Births	Per Cent (%) Live Births	Stillbirths	Stillbirth Rate	Early Neonatal Deaths	Early Neonatal Rate	Perinatal Mortality Rate	Adjusted PMR
0	24,301	40.6	155	6.3	73	3.0	9.3	6.8
1	19,055	31.8	75	3.9	32	1.7	5.6	3.7
2	10,128	16.9	41	4.0	30	3.0	7.0	4.4
3	3,925	6.6	32	8.1	9	2.3	10.4	7.1
4	1,462	2.4	13	8.8	7	4.8	13.6	9.5
5	545	0.9	1	1.8	3	5.5	7.3	5.5
6	237	0.4	2	8.4	1	4.2	12.6	4.2
More than 6	179	0.3	8	42.8	1	5.6	48.1	48.1
Not Stated	5	0.0	0	0.0	0	0.0	0.0	0.0
Total	**59,837**	**100.0**	**327**	**5.4**	**156**	**2.6**	**8.0**	**5.6**

Figure 3.1

Perinatal Mortality Rates by Age of Mother, 2003

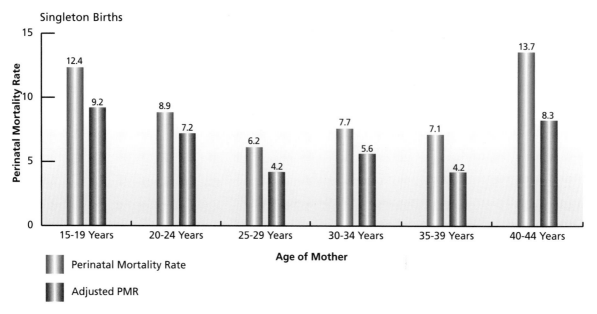

Note: See Table 3.1 for data. The adjusted rate excludes all deaths due to congenital anomalies. Categories where rates would be based on <100 Live Births are not included in this graph.

Figure 3.2

Percentage Distribution of Parity by Age of Mother, 2003

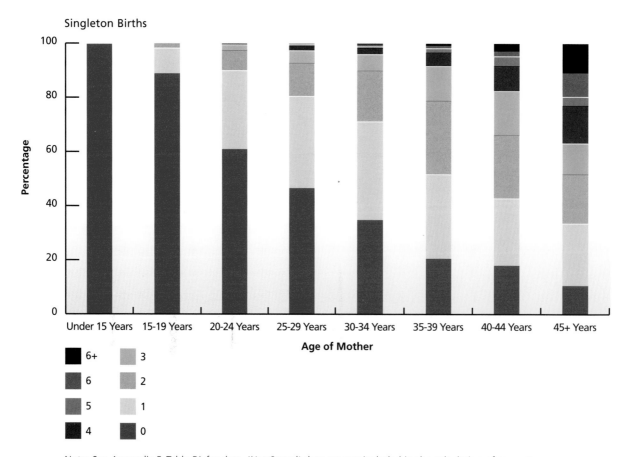

Note: See Appendix F, Table F1 for data. 'Not Stated' data are not included in the calculation of percentages.

Table 3.3
Marital Status

Live Births, Stillbirths, Early Neonatal Deaths and Mortality Rates, 2003

Singleton Births

Marital Status	Live Births	Per Cent (%) Live Births	Stillbirths	Stillbirth Rate	Early Neonatal Deaths	Early Neonatal Rate	Perinatal Mortality Rate	Adjusted PMR
Married	40,785	68.2	204	5.0	98	2.4	7.4	4.8
Single	18,126	30.3	113	6.2	55	3.0	9.2	7.2
Widowed	61	0.1	0	0.0	0	0.0	0.0	0.0
Separated	664	1.1	7	10.4	2	3.0	13.4	9.0
Divorced	196	0.3	2	10.1	1	5.1	15.2	10.2
Not Stated	5	0.0	1	166.7	0	0.0	166.7	166.7
Total	**59,837**	**100.0**	**327**	**5.4**	**156**	**2.6**	**8.0**	**5.6**

Figure 3.3
Mother's Age: Percentage Distribution of Singleton Births for Married and Single Status, 2003

Singleton Births

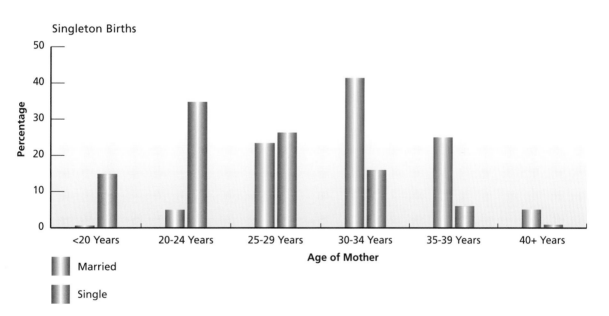

Note: See Appendix F, Table F3 for data. 'Not Stated' data are not included in the calculation of percentages.

Table 3.4
Father's Occupation

Live Births, Stillbirths, Early Neonatal Deaths and Mortality Rates, 2003

Singleton Births

Father's Occupation	Live Births	Per Cent (%) Live Births	Stillbirths	Stillbirth Rate	Early Neonatal Deaths	Early Neonatal Rate	Perinatal Mortality Rate	Adjusted PMR
Farmers & Farm Managers	2,547	4.3	13	5.1	6	2.4	7.4	4.3
Other Agricultural Occupations & Fishermen	579	1.0	1	1.7	1	1.7	3.4	3.4
Higher-Professional	3,780	6.3	12	3.2	4	1.1	4.2	3.2
Lower-Professional	2,995	5.0	12	4.0	5	1.7	5.7	4.0
Managers	4,850	8.1	23	4.7	8	1.6	6.4	3.3
Salaried-Employees	1,542	2.6	15	9.6	3	1.9	11.6	7.7
Non-Manual Workers	4,222	7.1	15	3.5	7	1.7	5.2	3.1
Other Non-Manual Workers	4,756	7.9	21	4.4	14	2.9	7.3	5.0
Skilled Manual Workers	10,949	18.3	43	3.9	33	3.0	6.9	3.8
Semi-skilled Manual Workers	2,589	4.3	11	4.2	3	1.2	5.4	3.9
Unskilled Manual Workers	549	0.9	6	10.8	1	1.8	12.6	9.0
Unemployed	2,129	3.6	13	6.1	11	5.2	11.2	8.0
Not Classifiable	976	1.6	6	6.1	3	3.1	9.2	8.2
Not Applicable	15,908	26.6	111	6.9	52	3.3	10.2	7.9
Not Stated	1,466	2.4	25	16.8	5	3.4	20.1	16.8
Total	**59,837**	**100.0**	**327**	**5.4**	**156**	**2.6**	**8.0**	**5.6**

Note: In this table 'Not Classifiable' includes 89 Fathers whose occupation was recorded as 'Home Duties'. See Appendix C for a description of the classification system for occupations.

Figure 3.4
Perinatal Mortality Rates by Father's Occupation, 2003

Singleton Births

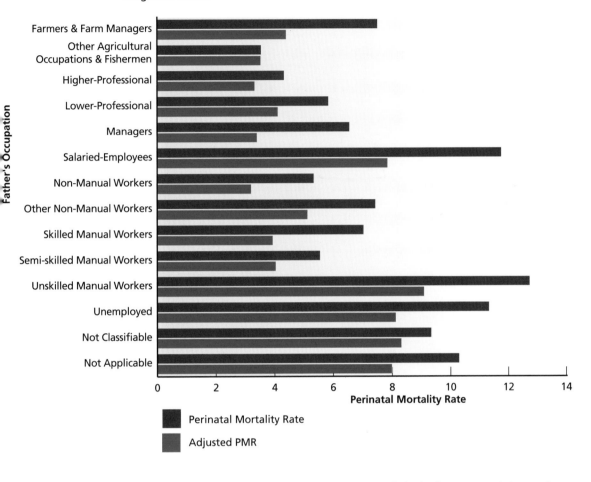

Perinatal Mortality Rate

Adjusted PMR

Note: See Table 3.4 for data. The adjusted rate excludes all deaths due to congenital anomalies.

Table 3.5
Mother's Occupation

Live Births, Stillbirths, Early Neonatal Deaths and Mortality Rates, 2003

Singleton Births

Mother's Occupation	Live Births	Per Cent (%) Live Births	Stillbirths	Stillbirth Rate	Early Neonatal Deaths	Early Neonatal Rate	Perinatal Mortality Rate	Adjusted PMR
Farmers & Farm Managers	104	0.2	2	18.9	0	0.0	18.9	18.9
Other Agricultural Occupations & Fishermen	138	0.2	0	0.0	2	14.5	14.5	7.3
Higher-Professional	2,677	4.5	7	2.6	6	2.2	4.8	2.6
Lower-Professional	7,447	12.4	33	4.4	12	1.6	6.0	4.2
Managers	3,611	6.0	12	3.3	13	3.6	6.9	3.0
Salaried-Employees	924	1.5	7	7.5	3	3.2	10.7	6.5
Non-Manual Workers	13,297	22.2	46	3.4	31	2.3	5.8	3.5
Other Non-Manual Workers	6,066	10.1	30	4.9	16	2.6	7.5	5.4
Skilled Manual Workers	665	1.1	1	1.5	1	1.5	3.0	1.5
Semi-skilled Manual Workers	2,742	4.6	15	5.4	7	2.6	8.0	5.8
Unskilled Manual Workers	6	0.0	2	250.0	0	0.0	250.0	250.0
Unemployed	2,810	4.7	17	6.0	13	4.6	10.6	8.5
Not Classifiable	2,110	3.5	21	9.9	2	0.9	10.8	9.9
Home Duties	16,300	27.2	115	7.0	44	2.7	9.7	6.9
Not Stated	940	1.6	19	19.8	6	6.4	26.1	23.0
Total	**59,837**	**100.0**	**327**	**5.4**	**156**	**2.6**	**8.0**	**5.6**

Note: 'Not Applicable' is not used in the classification of maternal occupation. See Appendix C for a description of the classification system for occupations.

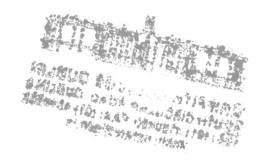

Figure 3.5
Perinatal Mortality Rates by Mother's Occupation, 2003

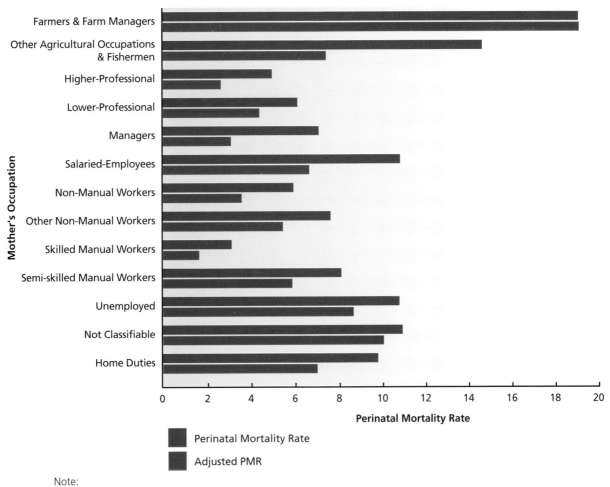

Singleton Births

Y-axis label: Mother's Occupation
X-axis label: Perinatal Mortality Rate

■ Perinatal Mortality Rate
■ Adjusted PMR

Note:
-See Table 3.5 for data. The adjusted rate excludes all deaths due to congenital anomalies.
-Categories where rates would be based on < 100 Live Births are not included in this graph.

Table 3.6

Number of Previous Stillbirths

(for women having second and subsequent births)

Live births, Stillbirths, Early Neonatal Deaths
and Mortality Rates, 2003

Singleton Births

Previous Stillbirths	Live Births	Per Cent (%) Live Births	Stillbirths	Stillbirth Rate	Early Neonatal Deaths	Early Neonatal Rate	Perinatal Mortality Rate	Adjusted PMR
0	34,881	98.2	163	4.7	80	2.3	6.9	4.5
1	602	1.7	7	11.5	2	3.3	14.8	13.2
2	34	0.1	0	0.0	0	0.0	0.0	0.0
3 and over	15	0.0	2	117.6	1	66.7	176.5	176.5
Not Stated	4	0.0	0	0.0	0	0.0	0.0	0.0
Total	**35,536**	**100.0**	**172**	**4.8**	**83**	**2.3**	**7.1**	**4.8**

Note: Primiparae (i.e. women with no previous live births or stillbirths) are not included in this table.

Table 3.7

Birthweight – All Singleton Births

Live Births, Stillbirths, Early Neonatal Deaths
and Mortality Rates, 2003

Birthweight (grams)	Live Births	Per Cent (%) Live Births	Stillbirths	Stillbirth Rate	Early Neonatal Deaths	Early Neonatal Rate	Perinatal Mortality Rate	Adjusted PMR
500-749	63	0.1	40	388.3	32	507.9	699.0	666.7
750-999	74	0.1	29	281.6	14	189.2	417.5	310.3
1000-1249	100	0.2	27	212.6	13	130.0	315.0	201.8
1250-1499	123	0.2	23	157.5	11	89.4	232.9	170.4
1500-1999	488	0.8	44	82.7	25	51.2	129.7	75.8
2000-2499	1,467	2.5	34	22.7	17	11.6	34.0	21.6
2500-2999	6,476	10.8	51	7.8	19	2.9	10.7	8.0
3000-3499	19,838	33.2	40	2.0	11	0.6	2.6	2.1
3500-3999	20,830	34.8	20	1.0	6	0.3	1.2	0.9
4000-4499	8,634	14.4	13	1.5	3	0.3	1.9	1.6
4500 and over	1,734	2.9	4	2.3	3	1.7	4.0	2.3
Not Stated	10	0.0	2	166.7	2	200.0	333.3	200.0
Total	**59,837**	**100.0**	**327**	**5.4**	**156**	**2.6**	**8.0**	**5.6**

Figure 3.6

Percentage Distribution of Live Births across Birthweight Groups, 2003

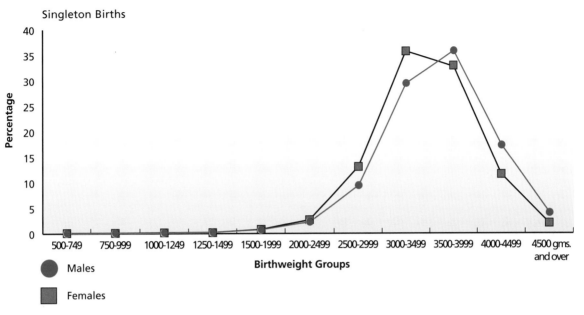

Singleton Births

Males

Females

Note:
- See Tables 3.8 and 3.9 for data.
- This figure does not include 1 birth for which the sex was recorded as 'indeterminate' or 'unknown'.
- 'Not Stated' data are not included in the calculation of percentages.

Table 3.8

Birthweight – Males

Live Births, Stillbirths, Early Neonatal Deaths
and Mortality Rates, 2003

Singleton Births

Birthweight (grams)	Live Births	Per Cent (%) Live Births	Stillbirths	Stillbirth Rate	Early Neonatal Deaths	Early Neonatal Rate	Perinatal Mortality Rate	Adjusted PMR
500-749	32	0.1	16	333.3	19	593.8	729.2	704.5
750-999	39	0.1	18	315.8	11	282.1	508.8	416.7
1000-1249	56	0.2	15	211.3	9	160.7	338.0	216.7
1250-1499	62	0.2	14	184.2	8	129.0	289.5	205.9
1500-1999	255	0.8	24	86.0	14	54.9	136.2	87.1
2000-2499	677	2.2	17	24.5	10	14.8	38.9	27.7
2500-2999	2,787	9.1	30	10.6	10	3.6	14.2	10.7
3000-3499	9,278	30.3	19	2.0	8	0.9	2.9	2.3
3500-3999	11,082	36.2	11	1.0	5	0.5	1.4	1.1
4000-4499	5,203	17.0	9	1.7	2	0.4	2.1	1.7
4500 and over	1,155	3.8	4	3.5	1	0.9	4.3	3.5
Not Stated	8	0.0	0	0.0	2	250.0	250.0	142.9
Total	**30,634**	**100.0**	**177**	**5.7**	**99**	**3.2**	**9.0**	**6.4**

Note: The 2003 dataset includes 1 singleton birth for which the sex was recorded as 'indeterminate' or 'unknown'. This birth is excluded from Tables 3.8 and 3.9.

Table 3.9

Birthweight – Females

Live Births, Stillbirths, Early Neonatal Deaths
and Mortality Rates, 2003

Singleton Births

Birthweight (grams)	Live Births	Per Cent (%) Live Births	Stillbirths	Stillbirth Rate	Early Neonatal Deaths	Early Neonatal Rate	Perinatal Mortality Rate	Adjusted PMR
500-749	31	0.1	24	436.4	13	419.4	672.7	632.7
750-999	35	0.1	10	222.2	3	85.7	288.9	179.5
1000-1249	44	0.2	12	214.3	4	90.9	285.7	183.7
1250-1499	61	0.2	9	128.6	3	49.2	171.4	134.3
1500-1999	233	0.8	20	79.1	11	47.2	122.5	63.3
2000-2499	790	2.7	17	21.1	7	8.9	29.7	16.3
2500-2999	3,689	12.6	21	5.7	9	2.4	8.1	5.9
3000-3499	10,560	36.2	21	2.0	3	0.3	2.3	1.9
3500-3999	9,748	33.4	9	0.9	1	0.1	1.0	0.7
4000-4499	3,431	11.7	4	1.2	1	0.3	1.5	1.5
4500 and over	579	2.0	0	0.0	2	3.5	3.5	0.0
Not Stated	2	0.0	2	500.0	0	0.0	500.0	333.3
Total	**29,203**	**100.0**	**149**	**5.1**	**57**	**2.0**	**7.0**	**4.7**

Note: The 2003 dataset includes 1 singleton birth for which the sex was recorded as 'indeterminate' or 'unknown'. This birth is excluded from Tables 3.8 and 3.9.

Figure 3.7 (A)

Perinatal Mortality Rates for Males and Females by Birthweight (500g – 2499grams), 2003

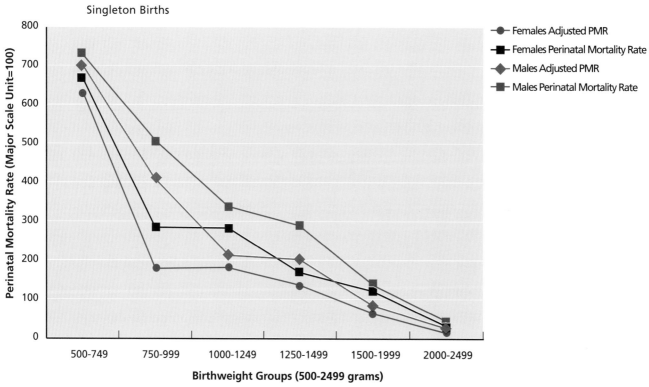

Singleton Births

Note:
- See Tables 3.8 and 3.9 for data.
- This figure does not include 1 birth for which the sex was recorded as 'indeterminate' or 'unknown'.

Figure 3.7 (B)
Perinatal Mortality Rates for Males and Females by Birthweight (2500 - 4500grams and over), 2003

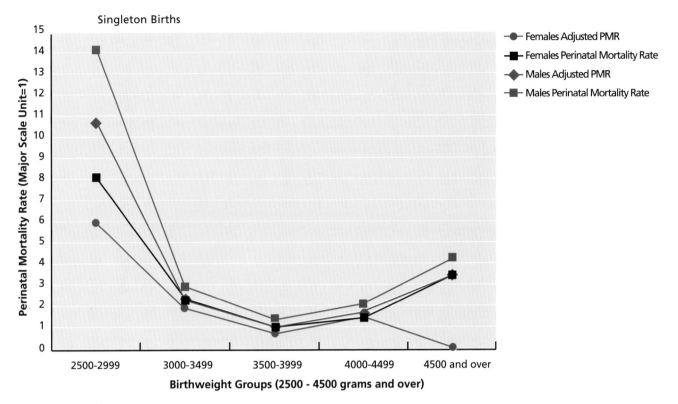

Note:
- See Tables 3.8 and 3.9 for data.
- This figure does not include 5 births for which the sex was recorded as 'indeterminate' or 'unknown'.

Table 3.10
Gestation Period at Delivery

Live Births, Stillbirths, Early Neonatal Deaths
and Mortality Rates, 2003

Singleton Births

Gestation Period (weeks)	Live Births	Per Cent (%) Live Births	Stillbirths	Stillbirth Rate	Early Neonatal Deaths	Early Neonatal Rate	Perinatal Mortality Rate	Adjusted PMR
Less than 22	1	0.0	2	666.7	1	1000.0	1000.0	1000.0
22-27	132	0.2	51	278.7	45	340.9	524.6	479.0
28-31	276	0.5	53	161.1	23	83.3	231.0	156.7
32-36	2,169	3.6	75	33.4	32	14.8	47.7	30.8
37-41	54,123	90.5	137	2.5	53	1.0	3.5	2.4
42 and over	3,124	5.2	7	2.2	1	0.3	2.6	1.6
Not Stated	12	0.0	2	142.9	1	83.3	214.3	214.3
Total	59,837	100.0	327	5.4	156	2.6	8.0	5.6

Figure 3.8
Perinatal Mortality Rates by Gestation Period, 2003

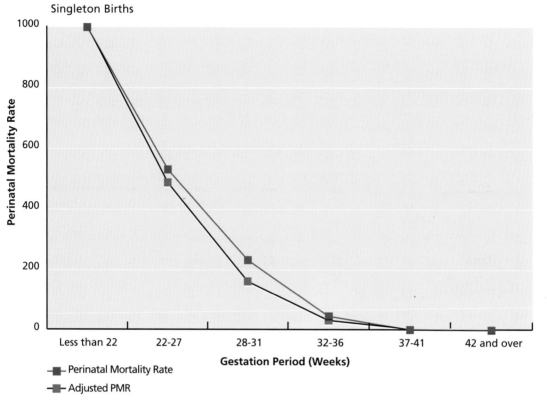

Singleton Births

Note: See Table 3.10 for data.

Table 3.11
Interval in Years Since Last Birth

Live Births, Stillbirths, Early Neonatal Deaths
and Mortality Rates, 2003

Singleton Births

Interval Since Last Birth	Live Births	Per Cent (%) Live Births	Stillbirths	Stillbirth Rate	Early Neonatal Deaths	Early Neonatal Rate	Perinatal Mortality Rate	Adjusted PMR
No Previous Births	24,301	40.6	155	6.3	73	3.0	9.3	6.8
1 year or less	552	0.9	10	17.8	4	7.2	24.9	17.9
>1 year to 2 years	8,634	14.4	43	5.0	18	2.1	7.0	4.4
>2 years to 3 years	8,941	14.9	31	3.5	14	1.6	5.0	3.6
>3 years to 4 years	5,656	9.5	25	4.4	13	2.3	6.7	4.4
>4 years to 5 years	3,556	5.9	14	3.9	8	2.2	6.2	3.1
>5 years to 6 years	2,318	3.9	10	4.3	3	1.3	5.6	4.3
More than 6 years	5,270	8.8	30	5.7	15	2.8	8.5	5.9
Number of Previous Births Unknown	2	0.0	0	0.0	0	0.0	0.0	0.0
Not Stated	607	1.0	9	14.6	8	13.2	27.6	21.2
Total	**59,837**	**100.0**	**327**	**5.4**	**156**	**2.6**	**8.0**	**5.6**

Table 3.12
Month of Birth

Live Births, Stillbirths, Early Neonatal Deaths
and Mortality Rates, 2003

Singleton Births

Month of Birth	Live Births	Per Cent (%) Live Births	Stillbirths	Stillbirth Rate	Early Neonatal Deaths	Early Neonatal Rate	Perinatal Mortality Rate	Adjusted PMR
January	4,862	8.1	24	4.9	12	2.5	7.4	4.5
February	4,438	7.4	22	4.9	9	2.0	7.0	4.7
March	5,124	8.6	29	5.6	20	3.9	9.5	6.6
April	4,956	8.3	23	4.6	16	3.2	7.8	5.6
May	5,238	8.8	21	4.0	10	1.9	5.9	4.4
June	5,041	8.4	36	7.1	18	3.6	10.6	7.9
July	5,302	8.9	35	6.6	17	3.2	9.7	6.4
August	5,048	8.4	31	6.1	16	3.2	9.3	6.7
September	5,143	8.6	26	5.0	11	2.1	7.2	4.8
October	5,117	8.6	30	5.8	12	2.3	8.2	5.6
November	4,682	7.8	21	4.5	3	0.6	5.1	3.6
December	4,886	8.2	29	5.9	12	2.5	8.3	5.9
Total	**59,837**	**100.0**	**327**	**5.4**	**156**	**2.6**	**8.0**	**5.6**

Table 3.13
Mother's Health Board of Residence

Live Births, Stillbirths, Early Neonatal Deaths
and Mortality Rates, 2003

Singleton Births

Mother's Health Board of Residence	Live Births	Per Cent (%) Live Births	Stillbirths	Stillbirth Rate	Early Neonatal Deaths	Early Neonatal Rate	Perinatal Mortality Rate	Adjusted PMR
Eastern	22,635	37.8	127	5.6	65	2.9	8.4	5.7
Midland	3,615	6.0	22	6.0	8	2.2	8.2	5.8
Mid-Western	4,941	8.3	25	5.0	10	2.0	7.0	5.4
North-Eastern	5,534	9.2	34	6.1	10	1.8	7.9	4.9
North-Western	3,030	5.1	14	4.6	13	4.3	8.9	7.2
South-Eastern	6,596	11.0	36	5.4	18	2.7	8.1	6.0
Southern	8,192	13.7	38	4.6	13	1.6	6.2	3.9
Western	5,268	8.8	29	5.5	18	3.4	8.9	6.4
Other	24	0.0	1	40.0	0	0.0	40.0	40.0
Unknown	2	0.0	1	333.3	1	500.0	666.7	666.7
Total	**59,837**	**100.0**	**327**	**5.4**	**156**	**2.6**	**8.0**	**5.6**

Note: See Appendix E for the classification system employed for county of residence.

Section 3
General Characteristics

Part 2 Multiple Births

Table 3.14

Maternities, Twins, Triplets and Twinning Rate for 2003

Births*	Maternities	Sets of Twins	Sets of Triplets	Twinning Rate
61,989	61,064	873	26	14.3

* Includes stillbirths.

Note: In 2003 there were 1,755 Twin births and 80 triplet births notified to the NPRS. Of these 10 births weighed <500 grams. In accordance with the WHO guidelines the National Perinatal Dataset includes only births weighing 500 grams or more. Therefore, for the purposes of this report, the number of *complete* sets of Twins is 873 and the number of *complete* sets of Triplets is 26.

See also Section 1, Introduction, Page 9.

Table 3.15

Age of Mother

Live Births, Stillbirths, Early Neonatal Deaths
and Mortality Rates, 2003

Multiple Births

Age of Mother	Live Births	Per Cent (%) Live Births	Stillbirths	Stillbirth Rate	Early Neonatal Deaths	Early Neonatal Rate	Perinatal Mortality Rate	Adjusted PMR
15-19 Years	43	2.4	0	0.0	1	23.3	23.3	0.0
20-24 Years	154	8.6	6	37.5	7	45.5	81.3	75.5
25-29 Years	380	21.2	4	10.4	3	7.9	18.2	18.2
30-34 Years	612	34.1	9	14.5	6	9.8	24.2	24.2
35-39 Years	541	30.1	10	18.1	3	5.5	23.6	23.6
40-44 Years	58	3.2	1	16.9	0	0.0	16.9	16.9
45 Years and over	6	0.3	0	0.0	1	166.7	166.7	0.0
Not Stated	1	0.1	0	0.0	0	0.0	0.0	0.0
Total	**1,795**	**100.0**	**30**	**16.4**	**21**	**11.7**	**27.9**	**26.3**

There were no multiple births to Mothers aged <15 years.

Table 3.16
Maternal Parity

Live Births, Stillbirths, Early Neonatal Deaths
and Mortality Rates, 2003

Multiple Births

Maternal Parity	Live Births	Per Cent (%) Live Births	Stillbirths	Stillbirth Rate	Early Neonatal Deaths	Early Neonatal Rate	Perinatal Mortality Rate	Adjusted PMR
0	741	41.3	20	26.3	10	13.5	39.4	36.9
1	616	34.3	4	6.5	7	11.4	17.7	16.2
2	267	14.9	6	22.0	3	11.2	33.0	33.0
3	111	6.2	0	0.0	1	9.0	9.0	9.0
4	42	2.3	0	0.0	0	0.0	0.0	0.0
5	12	0.7	0	0.0	0	0.0	0.0	0.0
6	4	0.2	0	0.0	0	0.0	0.0	0.0
More than 6	2	0.1	0	0.0	0	0.0	0.0	0.0
Total	**1,795**	**100.0**	**30**	**16.4**	**21**	**11.7**	**27.9**	**26.3**

Table 3.17
Marital Status

Live Births, Stillbirths, Early Neonatal Deaths
and Mortality Rates, 2003

Multiple Births

Marital Status	Live Births	Per Cent (%) Live Births	Stillbirths	Stillbirth Rate	Early Neonatal Deaths	Early Neonatal Rate	Perinatal Mortality Rate	Adjusted PMR
Married	1,377	76.7	21	15.0	14	10.2	25.0	23.6
Single	394	21.9	9	22.3	7	17.8	39.7	37.3
Widowed	2	0.1	0	0.0	0	0.0	0.0	0.0
Separated	16	0.9	0	0.0	0	0.0	0.0	0.0
Divorced	6	0.3	0	0.0	0	0.0	0.0	0.0
Total	**1,795**	**100.0**	**30**	**16.4**	**21**	**11.7**	**27.9**	**26.3**

Table 3.18
Father's Occupation

Live Births, Stillbirths, Early Neonatal Deaths
and Mortality Rates, 2003

Multiple Births

Father's Occupation	Live Births	Per Cent (%) Live Births	Stillbirths	Stillbirth Rate	Early Neonatal Deaths	Early Neonatal Rate	Perinatal Mortality Rate	Adjusted PMR
Farmers & Farm Managers	87	4.8	3	33.3	3	34.5	66.7	66.7
Other Agricultural Occupations & Fishermen	22	1.2	0	0.0	1	45.5	45.5	0.0
Higher-Professional	143	8.0	2	13.8	0	0.0	13.8	13.8
Lower-Professional	108	6.0	3	27.0	1	9.3	36.0	27.3
Managers	183	10.2	2	10.8	0	0.0	10.8	10.8
Salaried-Employees	58	3.2	0	0.0	0	0.0	0.0	0.0
Non-Manual Workers	132	7.4	2	14.9	1	7.6	22.4	22.4
Other Non-Manual Workers	150	8.4	0	0.0	0	0.0	0.0	0.0
Skilled Manual Workers	360	20.1	4	11.0	7	19.4	30.2	30.2
Semi-skilled Manual Workers	74	4.1	0	0.0	2	27.0	27.0	27.0
Unskilled Manual Workers	20	1.1	1	47.6	1	50.0	95.2	95.2
Unemployed	48	2.7	2	40.0	0	0.0	40.0	40.0
Not Classifiable	21	1.2	0	0.0	0	0.0	0.0	0.0
Not Applicable	334	18.6	9	26.2	5	15.0	40.8	38.0
Not Stated	55	3.1	2	35.1	0	0.0	35.1	35.1
Total	**1,795**	**100.0**	**30**	**16.4**	**21**	**11.7**	**27.9**	**26.3**

Note: In this table 'Not Classifiable' includes 1 Father whose occupation was recorded as 'Home Duties'.
See Appendix C for a description of the classification system for occupations.

Table 3.19
Mother's Occupation

Live Births, Stillbirths, Early Neonatal Deaths
and Mortality Rates, 2003

Multiple Births

Mother's Occupation	Live Births	Per Cent (%) Live Births	Stillbirths	Stillbirth Rate	Early Neonatal Deaths	Early Neonatal Rate	Perinatal Mortality Rate	Adjusted PMR
Farmers & Farm Managers	6	0.3	0	0.0	0	0.0	0.0	0.0
Higher-Professional	102	5.7	1	9.7	0	0.0	9.7	9.7
Lower-Professional	264	14.7	4	14.9	2	7.6	22.4	22.4
Managers	127	7.1	3	23.1	1	7.9	30.8	30.8
Salaried-Employees	18	1.0	0	0.0	1	55.6	55.6	55.6
Non-Manual Workers	401	22.3	9	22.0	4	10.0	31.7	31.7
Other Non-Manual Workers	181	10.1	4	21.6	3	16.6	37.8	27.3
Skilled Manual Workers	13	0.7	1	71.4	1	76.9	142.9	142.9
Semi-skilled Manual Workers	77	4.3	1	12.8	3	39.0	51.3	51.3
Unemployed	82	4.6	3	35.3	1	12.2	47.1	47.1
Not Classifiable	35	1.9	1	27.8	2	57.1	83.3	57.1
Home Duties	465	25.9	3	6.4	3	6.5	12.8	12.8
Not Stated	24	1.3	0	0.0	0	0.0	0.0	0.0
Total	**1,795**	**100.0**	**30**	**16.4**	**21**	**11.7**	**27.9**	**26.3**

Note: 'Not Applicable' is not used in the classification of maternal occupation. See Appendix C for a description of the classification system for occupations.

Table 3.20
Number of Previous Stillbirths
(for women having second and subsequent births)

Live Births, Stillbirths, Early Neonatal Deaths
and Mortality Rates, 2003

Multiple Births

Previous Stillbirths	Live Births	Per Cent (%) Live Births	Stillbirths	Stillbirth Rate	Early Neonatal Deaths	Early Neonatal Rate	Perinatal Rate Mortality	Adjusted PMR
0	1,032	97.9	10	9.6	11	10.7	20.2	19.2
1	20	1.9	0	0.0	0	0.0	0.0	0.0
2	2	0.2	0	0.0	0	0.0	0.0	0.0
Total	**1,054**	**100.0**	**10**	**9.4**	**11**	**10.4**	**19.7**	**18.8**

Note: Primiparae (i.e. women with no previous live births or stillbirths) are not included in this table.

Figure 3.9
Birthweights: Cumulative Percentages of Singleton and Multiple Live Births, 2003

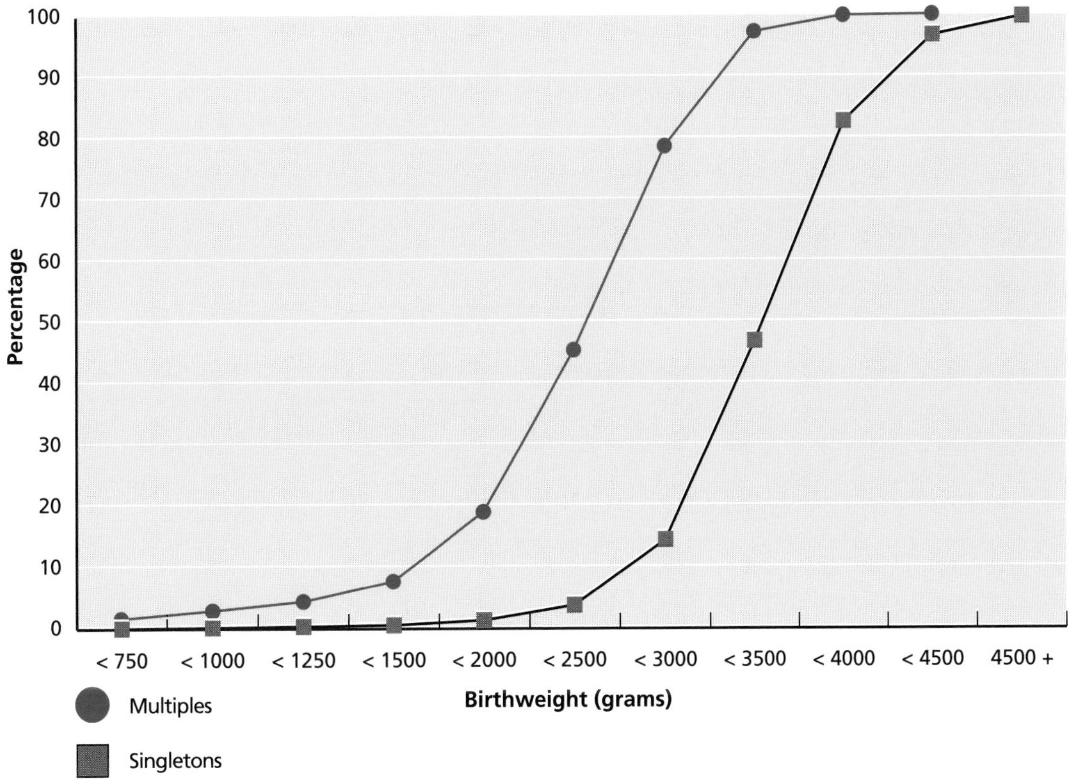

Note: Data are complied from Tables 3.7 and 3.21.

Table 3.21
Birthweight – All Multiple Births

Live Births, Stillbirths, Early Neonatal Deaths
and Mortality Rates, 2003

Birthweight (grams)	Live Births	Per Cent (%) Live Births	Stillbirths	Stillbirth Rate	Early Neonatal Deaths	Early Neonatal Rate	Perinatal Mortality Rate	Adjusted PMR
500-749	22	1.2	9	290.3	15	681.8	774.2	758.6
750-999	24	1.3	6	200.0	4	166.7	333.3	333.3
1000-1249	30	1.7	4	117.6	0	0.0	117.6	117.6
1250-1499	53	3.0	0	0.0	0	0.0	0.0	0.0
1500-1999	215	12.0	2	9.2	1	4.7	13.8	9.3
2000-2499	465	25.9	3	6.4	1	2.2	8.5	8.5
2500-2999	607	33.8	3	4.9	0	0.0	4.9	4.9
3000-3499	335	18.7	0	0.0	0	0.0	0.0	0.0
3500-3999	43	2.4	1	22.7	0	0.0	22.7	22.7
4000-4499	1	0.1	0	0.0	0	0.0	0.0	0.0
Not Stated	0	0.0	2	1000.0	0	0.0	1000.0	1000.0
Total	**1,795**	**100.0**	**30**	**16.4**	**21**	**11.7**	**27.9**	**26.3**

Table 3.22
Birthweight – Males

Live Births, Stillbirths, Early Neonatal Deaths
and Mortality Rates, 2003

Multiple Births

Birthweight (grams)	Live Births	Per Cent (%) Live Births	Stillbirths	Stillbirth Rate	Early Neonatal Deaths	Early Neonatal Rate	Perinatal Mortality Rate	Adjusted PMR
500-749	13	1.5	6	315.8	10	769.2	842.1	823.5
750-999	8	0.9	5	384.6	1	125.0	461.5	461.5
1000-1249	15	1.7	2	117.6	0	0.0	117.6	117.6
1250-1499	14	1.6	0	0.0	0	0.0	0.0	0.0
1500-1999	98	11.2	1	10.1	0	0.0	10.1	10.1
2000-2499	202	23.0	2	9.8	0	0.0	9.8	9.8
2500-2999	309	35.2	0	0.0	0	0.0	0.0	0.0
3000-3499	189	21.5	0	0.0	0	0.0	0.0	0.0
3500-3999	29	3.3	0	0.0	0	0.0	0.0	0.0
4000-4499	1	0.1	0	0.0	0	0.0	0.0	0.0
Not Stated	0	0.0	1	1000.0	0	0.0	1000.0	1000.0
Total	**878**	**100.0**	**17**	**19.0**	**11**	**12.5**	**31.3**	**29.1**

Note: The 2003 dataset includes 3 multiple births for which the sex was recorded as 'indeterminate' or 'unknown'.
These births are excluded from Tables 3.22 and 3.23.

Table 3.23
Birthweight – Females

Live Births, Stillbirths, Early Neonatal Deaths
and Mortality Rates, 2003

Multiple Births

Birthweight (grams)	Live Births	Per Cent (%) Live Births	Stillbirths	Stillbirth Rate	Early Neonatal Deaths	Early Neonatal Rate	Perinatal Mortality Rate	Adjusted PMR
500-749	9	1.0	3	250.0	5	555.6	666.7	666.7
750-999	16	1.8	1	58.8	3	187.5	235.3	235.3
1000-1249	15	1.6	2	117.6	0	0.0	117.6	117.6
1250-1499	37	4.0	0	0.0	0	0.0	0.0	0.0
1500-1999	116	12.7	1	8.5	1	8.6	17.1	8.6
2000-2499	263	28.8	1	3.8	1	3.8	7.6	7.6
2500-2999	298	32.6	3	10.0	0	0.0	10.0	10.0
3000-3499	146	16.0	0	0.0	0	0.0	0.0	0.0
3500-3999	14	1.5	1	66.7	0	0.0	66.7	66.7
Not Stated	0	0.0	1	1000.0	0	0.0	1000.0	1000.0
Total	**914**	**100.0**	**13**	**14.0**	**10**	**10.9**	**24.8**	**23.8**

Note: The 2003 dataset includes 3 multiple births for which the sex was recorded as 'indeterminate' or 'unknown'. These births are excluded from Tables 3.22 and 3.23.

Table 3.24
Gestation Period at Delivery

Live Births, Stillbirths, Early Neonatal Deaths
and Mortality Rates, 2003

Multiple Births

Gestation Period (weeks)	Live Births	Per Cent (%) Live Births	Stillbirths	Stillbirth Rate	Early Neonatal Deaths	Early Neonatal Rate	Perinatal Mortality Rate	Adjusted PMR
22-27	43	2.4	13	232.1	18	418.6	553.6	537.0
28-31	92	5.1	6	61.2	2	21.7	81.6	72.2
32-36	621	34.6	6	9.6	0	0.0	9.6	9.6
37-41	1,038	57.8	5	4.8	1	1.0	5.8	5.8
42 and over	1	0.1	0	0.0	0	0.0	0.0	0.0
Total	**1,795**	**100.0**	**30**	**16.4**	**21**	**11.7**	**27.9**	**26.3**

Table 3.25
Interval in Years Since Last Birth

Live Births, Stillbirths, Early Neonatal Deaths
and Mortality Rates, 2003

Multiple Births

Interval Since Last Birth	Live Births	Per Cent (%) Live Births	Stillbirths	Stillbirth Rate	Early Neonatal Deaths	Early Neonatal Rate	Perinatal Mortality Rate	Adjusted PMR
No Previous Births	741	41.3	20	26.3	10	13.5	39.4	36.9
1 year or less	26	1.4	2	71.4	1	38.5	107.1	107.1
>1 year to 2 years	224	12.5	3	13.2	8	35.7	48.5	48.5
>2 years to 3 years	247	13.8	0	0.0	0	0.0	0.0	0.0
>3 years to 4 years	181	10.1	2	10.9	0	0.0	10.9	10.9
>4 years to 5 years	124	6.9	3	23.6	0	0.0	23.6	23.6
>5 years to 6 years	89	5.0	0	0.0	1	11.2	11.2	11.2
More than 6 years	144	8.0	0	0.0	0	0.0	0.0	0.0
Not Stated	19	1.1	0	0.0	1	52.6	52.6	0.0
Total	**1,795**	**100.0**	**30**	**16.4**	**21**	**11.7**	**27.9**	**26.3**

Table 3.26
Month of Birth

Live Births, Stillbirths, Early Neonatal Deaths
and Mortality Rates, 2003

Multiple Births

Month of Birth	Live Births	Per Cent (%) Live Births	Stillbirths	Stillbirth Rate	Early Neonatal Deaths	Early Neonatal Rate	Perinatal Mortality Rate	Adjusted PMR
January	124	6.9	1	8.0	0	0.0	8.0	8.0
February	125	7.0	1	7.9	0	0.0	7.9	7.9
March	114	6.4	0	0.0	0	0.0	0.0	0.0
April	172	9.6	3	17.1	1	5.8	22.9	22.9
May	177	9.9	2	11.2	3	16.9	27.9	27.9
June	177	9.9	6	32.8	4	22.6	54.6	49.5
July	161	9.0	1	6.2	2	12.4	18.5	6.3
August	130	7.2	3	22.6	3	23.1	45.1	45.1
September	151	8.4	4	25.8	4	26.5	51.6	51.6
October	191	10.6	7	35.4	1	5.2	40.4	40.4
November	128	7.1	0	0.0	1	7.8	7.8	7.8
December	145	8.1	2	13.6	2	13.8	27.2	27.2
Total	**1,795**	**100.0**	**30**	**16.4**	**21**	**11.7**	**27.9**	**26.3**

Table 3.27
Mother's Health Board of Residence

Live Births, Stillbirths, Early Neonatal Deaths
and Mortality Rates, 2003

Multiple Births

Mother's Health Board of Residence	Live Births	Per Cent (%) Live Births	Stillbirths	Stillbirth Rate	Early Neonatal Deaths	Early Neonatal Rate	Perinatal Mortality Rate	Adjusted PMR
Eastern	702	39.1	15	20.9	10	14.2	34.9	34.9
Midland	86	4.8	1	11.5	0	0.0	11.5	11.5
Mid-Western	155	8.6	2	12.7	2	12.9	25.5	25.5
North-Eastern	129	7.2	1	7.7	2	15.5	23.1	23.1
North-Western	70	3.9	0	0.0	0	0.0	0.0	0.0
South-Eastern	225	12.5	1	4.4	0	0.0	4.4	4.4
Southern	257	14.3	5	19.1	3	11.7	30.5	26.8
Western	169	9.4	5	28.7	3	17.8	46.0	40.5
Other	2	0.1	0	0.0	1	500.0	500.0	0.0
Total	**1,795**	**100.0**	**30**	**16.4**	**21**	**11.7**	**27.9**	**26.3**

Note: See Appendix E for the classification system employed for county of residence.

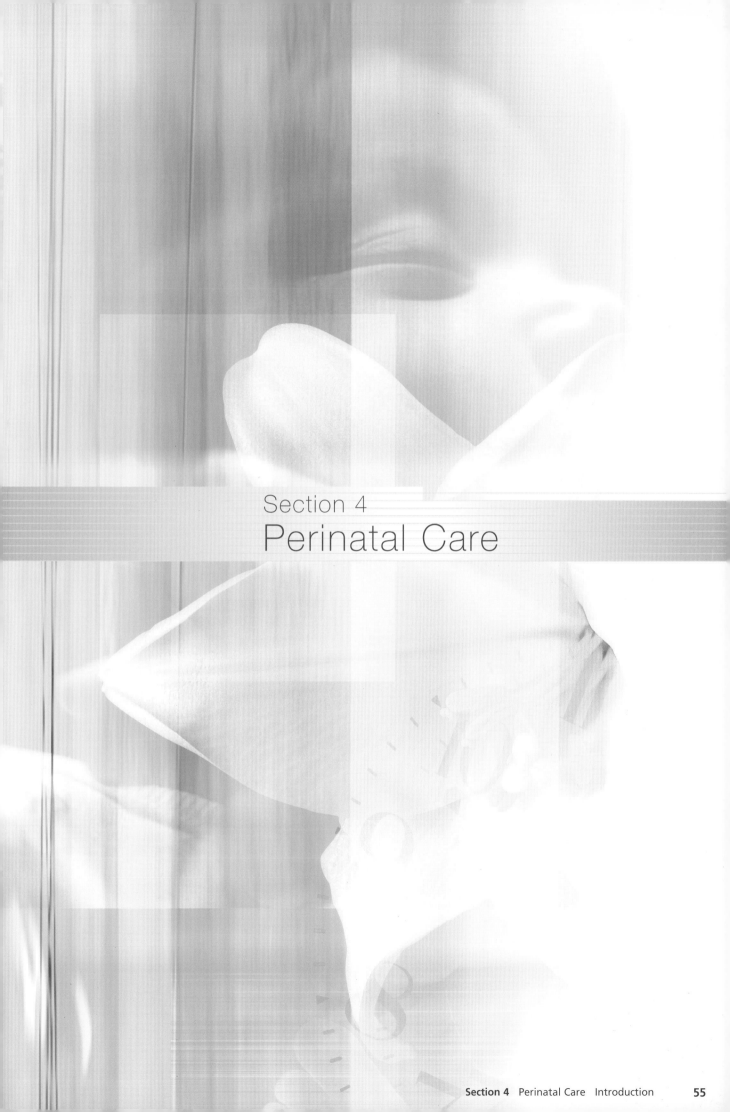

Section 4
Perinatal Care

This section presents a detailed review on aspects of perinatal care for the mother and infant. Part 1 reports on perinatal care for singleton births and Part 2 on multiple births. The following tables outline data for live births, stillbirths and early neonatal deaths, together with their corresponding rates. The perinatal mortality rate and adjusted perinatal mortality rate are also outlined in each table. Tables and figures are presented in some detail for a number of variables, including type of antenatal care; mother's length of stay; method of delivery; mother's immunity to rubella and type of feeding.

Section 4
Perinatal Care

Part 1 Singleton Births

Table 4.1
Type of Antenatal Care

Live Births, Stillbirths, Early Neonatal Deaths
and Mortality Rates, 2003

Singleton Births

Type of Antenatal Care	Live Births	Per Cent (%) Live Births	Stillbirths	Stillbirth Rate	Early Neonatal Deaths	Early Neonatal Rate	Perinatal Mortality Rate	Adjusted PMR
Hospital/Obstetrician	13,291	22.2	73	5.5	47	3.5	9.0	6.2
General Practitioner Only	191	0.3	3	15.5	2	10.5	25.8	15.6
Hospital and G.P. Combined	45,511	76.1	235	5.1	100	2.2	7.3	5.0
None	745	1.2	15	19.7	7	9.4	28.9	25.1
Midwife Only	93	0.2	0	0.0	0	0.0	0.0	0.0
Unknown	6	0.0	1	142.9	0	0.0	142.9	142.9
Total	**59,837**	**100.0**	**327**	**5.4**	**156**	**2.6**	**8.0**	**5.6**

Table 4.2
Mother's Length of Stay in Hospital Prior to Delivery

Live Births, Stillbirths, Early Neonatal Deaths
and Mortality Rates, 2003

Singleton Births

Antenatal Length of Stay	Live Births	Per Cent (%) Live Births	Stillbirths	Stillbirth Rate	Early Neonatal Deaths	Early Neonatal Rate	Perinatal Mortality Rate	Adjusted PMR
0-1 Days	53,444	89.7	268	5.0	119	2.2	7.2	5.0
2 Days	3,237	5.4	25	7.7	9	2.8	10.4	8.0
3-5 Days	1,828	3.1	22	11.9	12	6.6	18.4	11.4
6-8 Days	479	0.8	3	6.2	4	8.4	14.5	10.4
9-11 Days	186	0.3	3	15.9	5	26.9	42.3	26.9
12-14 Days	116	0.2	2	16.9	0	0.0	16.9	16.9
2 weeks or more	255	0.4	4	15.4	7	27.5	42.5	27.5
Not Stated	56	0.1	0	0.0	0	0.0	0.0	0.0
Total	**59,601**	**100.0**	**327**	**5.5**	**156**	**2.6**	**8.1**	**5.6**

Notes:
-'Not Stated' includes;
36 births where place of birth was recorded as domiciliary but birth was registered by a hospital. Mother was not admitted under a planned community midwife scheme, therefore, dates of mother's length of stay were not applicable.
10 births where place of birth was recorded as 'born before arrival'. Mother's admission date was after the infant's date of birth, therefore, antenatal length of stay was not applicable.
10 births where mother's admission date was not stated.
-Domiciliary births, of which there were 236, are excluded from this table. See Appendix H for detailed analysis.

Table 4.3
Mother's Length of Stay in Hospital After Delivery

Live Births, Stillbirths, Early Neonatal Deaths
and Mortality Rates, 2003

Singleton Births

Postnatal Length of Stay	Live Births	Per Cent (%) Live Births	Stillbirths	Stillbirth Rate	Early Neonatal Deaths	Early Neonatal Rate	Perinatal Mortality Rate	Adjusted PMR
0-1 Days	7,186	12.1	168	22.8	58	8.1	30.7	22.4
2 Days	16,099	27.0	73	4.5	32	2.0	6.5	4.1
3-5 Days	32,570	54.6	66	2.0	51	1.6	3.6	2.4
6-8 Days	3,208	5.4	13	4.0	7	2.2	6.2	5.0
9-11 Days	345	0.6	3	8.6	3	8.7	17.2	17.2
12-14 Days	75	0.1	2	26.0	2	26.7	51.9	26.7
2 weeks or more	67	0.1	1	14.7	1	14.9	29.4	29.4
Not Stated	51	0.1	1	19.2	2	39.2	57.7	57.7
Total	**59,601**	**100.0**	**327**	**5.5**	**156**	**2.6**	**8.1**	**5.6**

Note:
-'Not Stated' includes 36 births where place of birth was recorded as domiciliary but birth was registered by a hospital.
 Mother was not admitted under a planned community midwife scheme, therefore, dates of mother's length of stay were not applicable.
-Domiciliary births, of which there were 236, are excluded from this table. See Appendix H for detailed analysis.

Figure 4.1
Mother's Postnatal Length of Stay: Cumulative Percentages by Method of Delivery, 2003

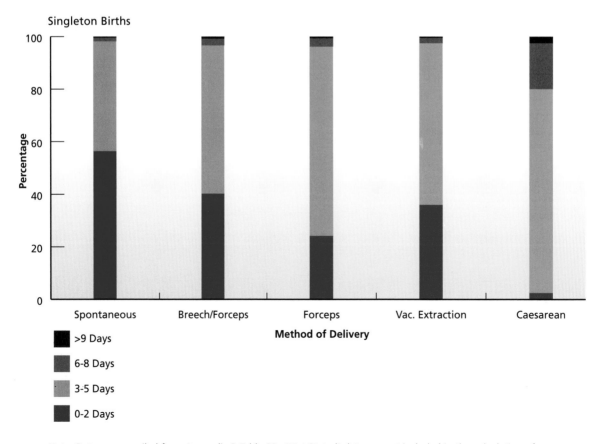

Note: Data are compiled from Appendix F, Table F9. 'Not Stated' data are not included in the calculation of percentages.

Table 4.4
Method of Delivery

Live Births, Stillbirths, Early Neonatal Deaths
and Mortality Rates, 2003

Singleton Births

Method of Delivery	Live Births	Per Cent (%) Live Births	Stillbirths	Stillbirth Rate	Early Neonatal Deaths	Early Neonatal Rate	Perinatal Mortality Rate	Adjusted PMR
Spontaneous	37,240	62.2	235	6.3	68	1.8	8.1	6.1
Breech/Forceps	224	0.4	34	131.8	14	62.5	186.0	132.2
Forceps	1,730	2.9	7	4.0	1	0.6	4.6	3.5
Vacuum Extraction	6,656	11.1	6	0.9	6	0.9	1.8	1.2
Caesarean	13,846	23.1	42	3.0	66	4.8	7.8	4.3
Other specified & Combined	133	0.2	2	14.8	1	7.5	22.2	14.9
Not Stated	8	0.0	1	111.1	0	0.0	111.1	0.0
Total	**59,837**	**100.0**	**327**	**5.4**	**156**	**2.6**	**8.0**	**5.6**

Table 4.5
Advance Hospital Bookings

Live Births, Stillbirths, Early Neonatal Deaths
and Mortality Rates, 2003

Singleton Births

Advance Hospital Bookings	Live Births	Per Cent (%) Live Births	Stillbirths	Stillbirth Rate	Early Neonatal Deaths	Early Neonatal Rate	Perinatal Mortality Rate	Adjusted PMR
Booked	58,136	97.5	299	5.1	141	2.4	7.5	5.2
Not Booked	1,427	2.4	28	19.2	15	10.5	29.6	23.5
Not Stated	38	0.0	0	0.0	0	0.0	0.0	0.0
Total	**59,601**	**100.0**	**327**	**5.5**	**156**	**2.6**	**8.1**	**5.6**

Note:
-'Not Stated' includes 33 births where place of birth was recorded as domiciliary but birth was registered by a hospital.
 Mother was not admitted under a planned community midwife scheme, therefore, hospital bookings were not applicable.
- Domiciliary births, of which there were 236, are excluded from this table. See Appendix H for detailed analysis.

Table 4.6

Size of Maternity Unit (number of live births and stillbirths annually)

Live Births, Stillbirths, Early Neonatal Deaths
and Mortality Rates, 2003

Size of Maternity Unit	Number of Hospitals	Live Births	Per Cent (%) Live Births	Stillbirths	Stillbirth Rate	Early Neonatal Deaths	Early Neonatal Rate	Perinatal Mortality Rate	Adjusted PMR
Less than 100	10	17	0.0	0	0.0	2	117.6	117.6	62.5
500-999	1	936	1.5	4	4.3	0	0.0	4.3	3.2
1000-1499	6	8,498	13.8	48	5.6	20	2.4	8.0	5.3
1500-1999	6	10,535	17.2	51	4.8	29	2.8	7.6	5.9
2000-3999	5	14,025	22.8	81	5.7	30	2.1	7.9	5.5
4000 and over	4	27,385	44.6	173	6.3	96	3.5	9.8	7.1
Total	**32**	**61,396**	**100.0**	**357**	**5.8**	**177**	**2.9**	**8.6**	**6.2**

Note: This table includes multiple births but excludes domiciliary births of which there were 236 in total.

Figure 4.2

Percentage of Live Births by Size of Maternity Unit, 2003

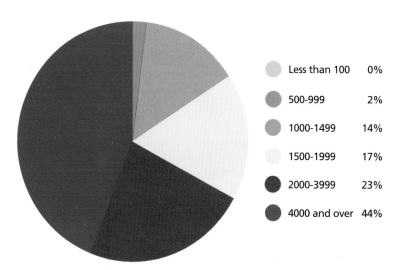

Less than 100   0%

500-999   2%

1000-1499   14%

1500-1999   17%

2000-3999   23%

4000 and over   44%

Note: See Table 4.6 for data. The size of unit refers to the number of live births and stillbirths occurring annually.

Table 4.7
Inter-Hospital Transfer of Infants

Live Births, Early Neonatal Deaths
and Mortality Rate, 2003

Singleton Births

Infant Transfers	Live Births	Per Cent (%) Live Births	Early Neonatal Deaths	Early Neonatal Rate
Transferred	363	0.6	12	33.1
Not Transferred	59,197	99.3	143	2.4
Not Stated	41	0.1	1	24.4
Total	**59,601**	**100.0**	**156**	**2.6**

Note:
- 'Not Stated' includes 32 births where place of birth was recorded as domiciliary but birth was registered by a hospital. Mother was not admitted under a planned community midwife scheme, therefore, transfer indicators were not applicable.
- Domiciliary births, of which there were 236, are excluded from this table. See Appendix H for detailed analysis.

Table 4.8
Rubella: Immune Status of Mother
Numbers and Percentages, 2003

Singleton Births

Rubella	Frequency	Per Cent (%)
Immune	52,552	87.4
Not Immune	2,009	3.3
Unknown	5,597	9.3
Not Stated	6	0.0
Total	**60,164**	**100.0**

Table 4.9
Age of Mother by Infant's Type of Feeding
Numbers and Percentages, 2003

Singleton Births

Age of Mother	Type of Feeding				
Frequency Row Per Cent Col. Per Cent	Artificial	Breast	Combined	Not Stated	Total
Under 15 Years	11	3	0	0	14
	78.57	21.43	0.00	0.00	
	0.03	0.01	0.00	0.00	0.02
15-19 Years	2,197	541	56	5	2,799
	78.49	19.33	2.00	0.18	
	6.67	2.18	2.78	5.75	4.68
20-24 Years	5,530	2,545	220	16	8,311
	66.54	30.62	2.65	0.19	
	16.79	10.27	10.92	18.39	13.89
25-29 Years	7,934	5,862	555	18	14,369
	55.22	40.80	3.86	0.13	
	24.08	23.65	27.54	20.69	24.01
30-34 Years	10,429	9,235	757	28	20,449
	51.00	45.16	3.70	0.14	
	31.66	37.25	37.57	32.18	34.17
35-39 Years	5,729	5,523	342	15	11,609
	49.35	47.58	2.95	0.13	
	17.39	22.28	16.97	17.24	19.40
40-44 Years	1,062	1,027	78	4	2,171
	48.92	47.31	3.59	0.18	
	3.22	4.14	3.87	4.60	3.63
45 Years and over	29	31	5	0	65
	44.62	47.69	7.69	0.00	
	0.09	0.13	0.25	0.00	0.11
Not Stated	24	23	2	1	50
	48.00	46.00	4.00	2.00	
	0.07	0.09	0.10	1.15	0.08
Total	32,945	24,790	2,015	87	59,837
	55.06	41.43	3.37	0.15	100.00

Note:
- See Appendix F for an explanation of the table format.
- 'Not Stated' contains 73 Early Neonatal Deaths for which Type of Feeding was not stated.

Figure 4.3
Percentage of Mothers Breastfeeding by Father's Occupation, 2003

Singleton Births

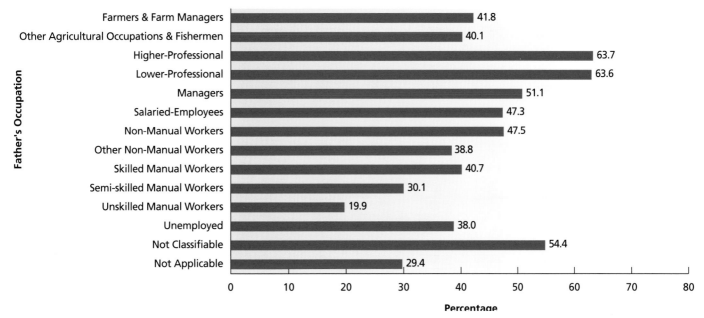

Note: Data are compiled from Appendix F, Table F15. 'Not Stated' data are not included in the calculation of percentages.

Figure 4.4
Percentage of Mothers Breastfeeding by Mother's Occupation, 2003

Singleton Births

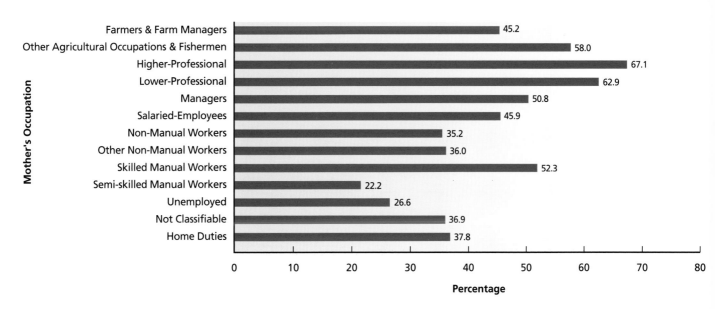

Note:
-Data are compiled from Appendix F, Table F16. 'Not Stated' data are not included in the calculation of percentages.
-Categories where percentages would be based on <50 births are not included in this graph.

Figure 4.5
Percentage of Mothers Breastfeeding by Age of Mother, 2003

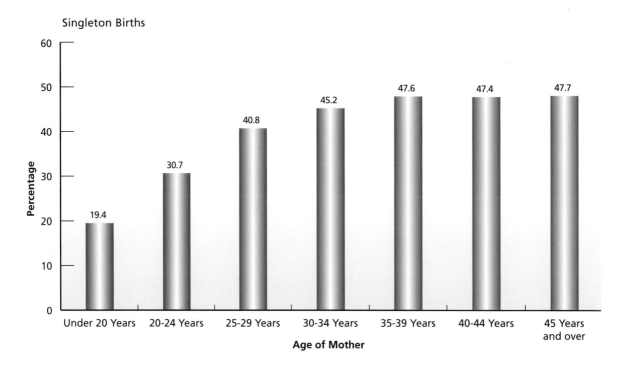

Singleton Births

Note: See Table 4.9 for data. 'Not Stated' data are not included in the calculation of percentages.

Section 4
Perinatal Care

Part 2 Multiple Births

Table 4.10
Type of Antenatal Care

Live Births, Stillbirths, Early Neonatal Deaths
and Mortality Rates, 2003

Multiple Births

Type of Antenatal Care	Live Births	Per Cent (%) Live Births	Stillbirths	Stillbirth Rate	Early Neonatal Deaths	Early Neonatal Rate	Perinatal Mortality Rate	Adjusted PMR
Hospital/Obstetrician	636	35.4	12	18.5	9	14.2	32.4	32.4
General Practitioner Only	3	0.2	0	0.0	0	0.0	0.0	0.0
Hospital and G.P. Combined	1,127	62.8	18	15.7	12	10.6	26.2	23.6
None	27	1.5	0	0.0	0	0.0	0.0	0.0
Midwife Only	2	0.1	0	0.0	0	0.0	0.0	0.0
Total	**1,795**	**100.0**	**30**	**16.4**	**21**	**11.7**	**27.9**	**26.3**

Table 4.11
Mother's Length of Stay in Hospital Prior to Delivery

Live Births, Stillbirths, Early Neonatal Deaths
and Mortality Rates, 2003

Multiple Births

Antenatal Length of Stay	Live Births	Per Cent (%) Live Births	Stillbirths	Stillbirth Rate	Early Neonatal Deaths	Early Neonatal Rate	Perinatal Mortality Rate	Adjusted PMR
0-1 Days	1,324	73.8	19	14.1	16	12.1	26.1	24.6
2 Days	133	7.4	1	7.5	2	15.0	22.4	22.4
3-5 Days	144	8.0	7	46.4	1	6.9	53.0	53.0
6-8 Days	74	4.1	1	13.3	1	13.5	26.7	13.5
9-11 Days	48	2.7	1	20.4	1	20.8	40.8	40.8
12-14 Days	23	1.3	0	0.0	0	0.0	0.0	0.0
2 weeks or more	49	2.7	1	20.0	0	0.0	20.0	20.0
Total	**1,795**	**100.0**	**30**	**16.4**	**21**	**11.7**	**27.9**	**26.3**

Note:There were no domiciliary multiple births.

Table 4.12
Mother's Length of Stay in Hospital After Delivery

Live Births, Stillbirths, Early Neonatal Deaths
and Mortality Rates, 2003

Multiple Births

Postnatal Length of Stay	Live Births	Per Cent (%) Live Births	Stillbirths	Stillbirth Rate	Early Neonatal Deaths	Early Neonatal Rate	Perinatal Mortality Rate	Adjusted PMR
0-1 Days	52	2.9	8	133.3	9	173.1	283.3	271.2
2 Days	99	5.5	3	29.4	3	30.3	58.8	49.5
3-5 Days	1,070	59.6	11	10.2	7	6.5	16.7	15.7
6-8 Days	481	26.8	4	8.2	2	4.2	12.4	12.4
9-11 Days	65	3.6	2	29.9	0	0.0	29.9	29.9
12-14 Days	14	0.8	1	66.7	0	0.0	66.7	66.7
2 weeks or more	13	0.7	1	71.4	0	0.0	71.4	71.4
Not Stated	1	0.1	0	0.0	0	0.0	0.0	0.0
Total	1,795	100.0	30	16.4	21	11.7	27.9	26.3

Note:There were no domiciliary multiple births.

Figure 4.6
Percentage Distribution of Births by Mother's Postnatal Length of Stay in Days, 2003

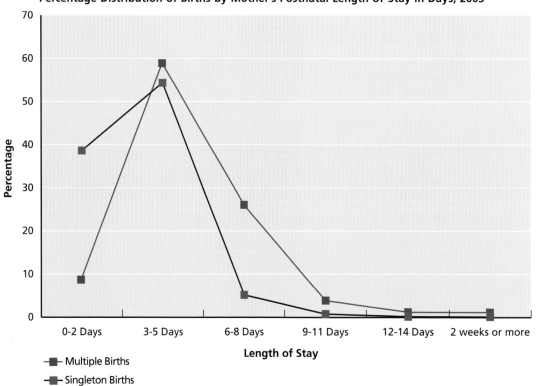

Note: Includes stillbirths. See Tables 4.3 and 4.12 for data. 'Not Stated' data are not included in the calculation of percentages.

Table 4.13
Method of Delivery

Live Births, Stillbirths, Early Neonatal Deaths
and Mortality Rates, 2003

Multiple Births

Method of Delivery	Live Births	Per Cent (%) Live Births	Stillbirths	Stillbirth Rate	Early Neonatal Deaths	Early Neonatal Rate	Perinatal Mortality Rate	Adjusted PMR
Spontaneous	472	26.3	11	22.8	9	19.1	41.4	39.4
Breech/Forceps	91	5.1	2	21.5	3	33.0	53.8	53.8
Forceps	28	1.6	0	0.0	0	0.0	0.0	0.0
Vacuum Extraction	146	8.1	0	0.0	0	0.0	0.0	0.0
Caesarean	1,047	58.3	16	15.1	9	8.6	23.5	21.7
Other specified & Combined	11	0.6	1	83.3	0	0.0	83.3	83.3
Total	**1,795**	**100.0**	**30**	**16.4**	**21**	**11.7**	**27.9**	**26.3**

Table 4.14
Advance Hospital Bookings

Live Births, Stillbirths, Early Neonatal Deaths
and Mortality Rates, 2003

Multiple Births

Advance Hospital Bookings	Live Births	Per Cent (%) Live Births	Stillbirths	Stillbirth Rate	Early Neonatal Deaths	Early Neonatal Rate	Perinatal Mortality Rate	Adjusted PMR
Booked	1,746	97.3	29	16.3	20	11.5	27.6	26.0
Not Booked	49	2.7	1	20.0	1	20.4	40.0	40.0
Total	**1,795**	**100.0**	**30**	**16.4**	**21**	**11.7**	**27.9**	**26.3**

Note:There were no domiciliary multiple births.

Table 4.15
Inter-Hospital Transfer of Infants

Live Births, Early Neonatal Deaths
and Mortality Rate, 2003

Multiple Births

Infant Transfers	Live Births	Per Cent (%) Live Births	Early Neonatal Deaths	Early Neonatal Rate
Transferred	54	3.0	1	18.5
Not Transferred	1,741	97.0	20	11.5
Total	**1,795**	**100.0**	**21**	**11.7**

Note:There were no domiciliary multiple births.

Table 4.16
Rubella: Immune Status of Mother
Numbers and Percentages, 2003

Multiple Births

Rubella	Frequency	Per Cent (%)
Immune	1,529	83.8
Not Immune	54	3.0
Unknown	242	13.3
Total	1,825	100.0

Table 4.17
Age of Mother by Infant's Type of Feeding
Numbers and Percentages, 2003

Multiple Births

Age of Mother	Type of Feeding				
Frequency Row Per Cent Col. Per Cent	Artificial	Breast	Combined	Not Stated	Total
15-19 Years	30	12	0	1	43
	69.77	27.91	0.00	2.33	
	2.69	2.44	0.00	5.88	2.40
20-24 Years	96	45	7	6	154
	62.34	29.22	4.55	3.90	
	8.61	9.16	4.07	35.29	8.58
25-29 Years	249	86	44	1	380
	65.53	22.63	11.58	0.26	
	22.33	17.52	25.58	5.88	21.17
30-34 Years	402	148	56	6	612
	65.69	24.18	9.15	0.98	
	36.05	30.14	32.56	35.29	34.09
35-39 Years	306	175	57	3	541
	56.56	32.35	10.54	0.55	
	27.44	35.64	33.14	17.65	30.14
40-44 Years	31	21	6	0	58
	53.45	36.21	10.34	0.00	
	2.78	4.28	3.49	0.00	3.23
45 Years and over	1	3	2	0	6
	16.67	50.00	33.33	0.00	
	0.09	0.61	1.16	0.00	0.33
Not Stated	0	1	0	0	1
	0.00	100.00	0.00	0.00	
	0.00	0.20	0.00	0.00	0.06
Total	1,115	491	172	17	1,795
	62.12	27.35	9.58	0.95	100.00

Note:
- See Appendix F for an explanation of the table format.
- 'Not Stated' contains 11 Early Neonatal Deaths for which Type of Feeding was not stated.

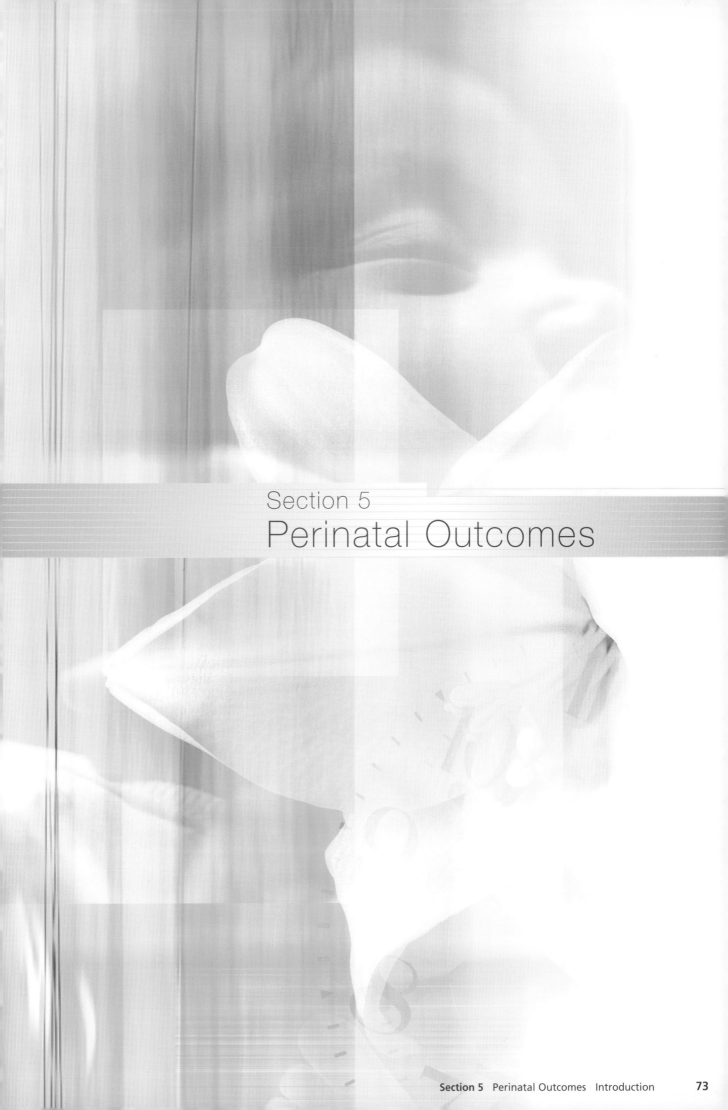

Section 5
Perinatal Outcomes

This section presents a detailed review on aspects of perinatal outcomes for the infant. Part 1 reports on perinatal outcomes for singleton births and Part 2 on multiple births. Cause of death is examined in greater detail according to the guidelines set out by the World Health Organisation in the ninth revision of the International Classification of Diseases. The following tables outline data for live births, antepartum and intrapartum stillbirths and early neonatal deaths, together with their corresponding rates. Mortality numbers and rates are presented by birthweight and cause of death. Age at death for early neonatal deaths and post-mortem analysis are also outlined.

Section 5
Perinatal Outcomes

Part 1 Singleton Births

Table 5.1
**Live Births, Antepartum and Intrapartum Stillbirths, Early Neonatal Deaths
and Mortality Rates by Birthweight, 2003**

Singleton Births

Birthweight (grams)	Live Births	Per Cent (%) Live Births	Ante-partum Stillbirths	Intra-partum Stillbirths	Not Stated	Stillbirth Rate	Early Neonatal Deaths	Early Neonatal Rate	Perinatal Mortality Rate	Adjusted PMR
500-749	63	0.1	28	4	8	388.3	32	507.9	699.0	666.7
750-999	74	0.1	21	0	8	281.6	14	189.2	417.5	310.3
1000-1249	100	0.2	17	3	7	212.6	13	130.0	315.0	201.8
1250-1499	123	0.2	17	1	5	157.5	11	89.4	232.9	170.4
1500-1999	488	0.8	30	6	8	82.7	25	51.2	129.7	75.8
2000-2499	1,467	2.5	28	2	4	22.7	17	11.6	34.0	21.6
2500-2999	6,476	10.8	35	6	10	7.8	19	2.9	10.7	8.0
3000-3499	19,838	33.2	31	2	7	2.0	11	0.6	2.6	2.1
3500-3999	20,830	34.8	15	2	3	1.0	6	0.3	1.2	0.9
4000-4499	8,634	14.4	11	1	1	1.5	3	0.3	1.9	1.6
4500 and over	1,734	2.9	3	0	1	2.3	3	1.7	4.0	2.3
Not Stated	10	0.0	2	0	0	166.7	2	200.0	333.3	200.0
Total	59,837	100.0	238	27	62	5.4	156	2.6	8.0	5.6

Table 5.2
Stillbirths, Early Neonatal Deaths
and Mortality Rates by Cause of Death, 2003

Singleton Births

ICD Codes	Cause of Death	Stillbirths	Stillbirth Rate	Early Neonatal Deaths	Early Neonatal Rate	Total Deaths	Perinatal Mortality Rate
	Congenital Anomalies						
740	Anencephalus	14	0.23	9	0.15	23	0.38
741	Spina Bifida	0	0.00	1	0.02	1	0.02
742	Other Central Nervous System Anomalies	2	0.03	7	0.12	9	0.15
743	Other Congenital Anomalies	13	0.22	10	0.17	23	0.38
746	Other Congenital Anomalies of the Heart	7	0.12	11	0.18	18	0.30
748	Congenital Anomalies of Respiratory System	0	0.00	17	0.28	17	0.28
749.0-751.9	Cleft Palate & Lip, Other Digestive Anomalies	2	0.03	0	0.00	2	0.03
753	Congenital Anomalies of Urinary System	3	0.05	10	0.17	13	0.22
754.0-756.9	Musculoskeletal System	5	0.08	7	0.12	12	0.20
758	Chromosomal Anomalies including Downs Syndrome	9	0.15	20	0.33	29	0.48
	Maternal Conditions and Complications in Pregnancy						
760	Maternal Hypertensive Disorders	11	0.18	0	0.00	11	0.18
760.1-761.9	Other Maternal Complications	14	0.23	1	0.02	15	0.25
762	Placenta Praevia	1	0.02	0	0.00	1	0.02
762.1	Other Placental Separation and Haemorrhage	48	0.80	2	0.03	50	0.83
762.2	Other Morphological and Functional Anomalies of Placenta	21	0.35	0	0.00	21	0.35
762.4	Prolapsed Cord	2	0.03	0	0.00	2	0.03
762.5	Other Compression of Umbilical Cord	16	0.27	0	0.00	16	0.27
762.6-762.9	Other Complications of Placenta, Cord & Membrane	7	0.12	0	0.00	7	0.12
763.2-763.9	Other Complications of Labour/Delivery	1	0.02	1	0.02	2	0.03
	Slow Foetal Growth, Malnutrition & Immaturity						
764	Slow Foetal Growth & Malnutrition	8	0.13	1	0.02	9	0.15
765	Short Gestation and Low Birthweight	15	0.25	20	0.33	35	0.58
	Birth Trauma						
767	Birth Trauma	0	0.00	1	0.02	1	0.02
768	Intrauterine Hypoxia/Anoxia	29	0.48	4	0.07	33	0.55
769	Respiratory Distress Syndrome	0	0.00	3	0.05	3	0.05
770	Respiratory Conditions of Foetus/Newborn	3	0.05	8	0.13	11	0.18
	Other Foetal and Neonatal Conditions						
771	Perinatal Infections	6	0.10	5	0.08	11	0.18
772	Neonatal/Foetal Haemorrhage	3	0.05	5	0.08	8	0.13
775	Metabolic and Endocrine Disorders	1	0.02	2	0.03	3	0.05
778	Integument and Temperature Regulation	5	0.08	1	0.02	6	0.10
	Maceration, ill-Defined Conditions & All other Causes						
779.9	Maceration	5	0.08	0	0.00	5	0.08
780-796,799	Symptoms, Signs, and Ill-Defined Conditions	74	1.23	5	0.08	79*	1.31
	All Other Causes	2	0.03	5	0.08	7	0.12
Total		**327**	**5.44**	**156**	**2.61**	**483**	**8.03**

* Note: The significant number in this category is due to the absence of information on Principal Diagnosis in relation to 42 births in three particular hospitals.

Table 5.3

Perinatal Mortality, Numbers and Rates, by Birthweight and Cause of Death, 2003

Singleton Births

Birthweight (grams)	Anencephalus		Spina Bifida		Other Central Nervous System Abnormalities		Congenital Anomalies of the Heart		Chromosomal Anomalies		Other Congenital Anomalies	
	Number	Rate	Number	Rate	Number	Rate	Number	Rate	Number	Rate	Number	Rate
500-749	1	9.7	0	0.0	0	0.0	0	0.0	5	48.5	4	38.8
750-999	3	29.1	1	9.7	0	0.0	1	9.7	4	38.8	7	68.0
1000-1249	5	39.4	0	0.0	0	0.0	0	0.0	2	15.7	11	86.6
1250-1499	1	6.8	0	0.0	2	13.7	0	0.0	3	20.5	5	34.2
1500-1999	5	9.4	0	0.0	1	1.9	5	9.4	8	15.0	12	22.6
2000-2499	3	2.0	0	0.0	1	0.7	1	0.7	4	2.7	10	6.7
2500-2999	3	0.5	0	0.0	3	0.5	3	0.5	2	0.3	7	1.1
3000-3499	1	0.1	0	0.0	0	0.0	5	0.3	0	0.0	4	0.2
3500-3999	1	0.0	0	0.0	0	0.0	2	0.1	1	0.0	3	0.1
4000-4499	0	0.0	0	0.0	1	0.1	1	0.1	0	0.0	0	0.0
4500 and over	0	0.0	0	0.0	1	0.6	0	0.0	0	0.0	2	1.2
Not Stated	0	0.0	0	0.0	0	0.0	0	0.0	0	0.0	2	166.7
Total	**23**	**0.4**	**1**	**0.0**	**9**	**0.1**	**18**	**0.3**	**29**	**0.5**	**67**	**1.1**

Table 5.3 Continued

Perinatal Mortality, Numbers and Rates, by Birthweight and Cause of Death, 2003

Singleton Births

Birthweight (grams)	Maternal Complications		Placenta, Cord, Membranes		Other Complications of Labour		Slow Foetal Growth		Birth Trauma		Hypoxia/Anoxia	
	Number	Rate	Number	Rate	Number	Rate	Number	Rate	Number	Rate	Number	Rate
500-749	7	68.0	13	126.2	1	9.7	22	213.6	0	0.0	9	87.4
750-999	4	38.8	7	68.0	0	0.0	7	68.0	0	0.0	2	19.4
1000-1249	0	0.0	6	47.2	0	0.0	1	7.9	0	0.0	3	23.6
1250-1499	2	13.7	7	47.9	0	0.0	0	0.0	0	0.0	2	13.7
1500-1999	3	5.6	13	24.4	1	1.9	7	13.2	1	1.9	5	9.4
2000-2499	2	1.3	8	5.3	0	0.0	4	2.7	0	0.0	3	2.0
2500-2999	4	0.6	20	3.1	0	0.0	2	0.3	0	0.0	7	1.1
3000-3499	2	0.1	14	0.7	0	0.0	0	0.0	0	0.0	8	0.4
3500-3999	0	0.0	5	0.2	0	0.0	0	0.0	0	0.0	4	0.2
4000-4499	1	0.1	4	0.5	0	0.0	0	0.0	0	0.0	2	0.2
4500 and over	0	0.0	0	0.0	0	0.0	0	0.0	0	0.0	2	1.2
Not Stated	1	83.3	0	0.0	0	0.0	1	83.3	0	0.0	0	0.0
Total	**26**	**0.4**	**97**	**1.6**	**2**	**0.0**	**44**	**0.7**	**1**	**0.0**	**47**	**0.8**

Table 5.3 Continued
Perinatal Mortality, Numbers and Rates, by Birthweight and Cause of Death, 2003

Singleton Births

Birthweight (grams)	Perinatal Infections		Foetal/Neonatal Haemorrhage		Haemolytic Disease		Metabolic, Endocrine Disturbances		Integument, Temperature Regulations		Maceration	
	Number	Rate	Number	Rate	Number	Rate	Number	Rate	Number	Rate	Number	Rate
500-749	2	19.4	0	0.0	0	0.0	0	0.0	0	0.0	1	9.7
750-999	0	0.0	1	9.7	0	0.0	0	0.0	1	9.7	1	9.7
1000-1249	3	23.6	2	15.7	0	0.0	1	7.9	0	0.0	0	0.0
1250-1499	2	13.7	1	6.8	0	0.0	0	0.0	1	6.8	0	0.0
1500-1999	0	0.0	0	0.0	0	0.0	0	0.0	1	1.9	0	0.0
2000-2499	1	0.7	0	0.0	0	0.0	0	0.0	2	1.3	1	0.7
2500-2999	1	0.2	1	0.2	0	0.0	2	0.3	1	0.2	0	0.0
3000-3499	0	0.0	2	0.1	0	0.0	0	0.0	0	0.0	0	0.0
3500-3999	2	0.1	0	0.0	0	0.0	0	0.0	0	0.0	1	0.0
4000-4499	0	0.0	1	0.1	0	0.0	0	0.0	0	0.0	0	0.0
4500 and over	0	0.0	0	0.0	0	0.0	0	0.0	0	0.0	1	0.6
Not Stated	0	0.0	0	0.0	0	0.0	0	0.0	0	0.0	0	0.0
Total	11	0.2	8	0.1	0	0.0	3	0.0	6	0.1	5	0.1

Table 5.3 Continued
Perinatal Mortality, Numbers and Rates, by Birthweight and Cause of Death, 2003

Singleton Births

Birthweight (grams)	Symptoms, Signs and Ill-Defined Conditions		All Other Causes		Not Stated		All Causes of Perinatal Mortality	
	Number	Rate	Number	Rate	Number	Rate	Number	Rate
500-749	7	68.0	0	0.0	0	0.0	72	699.0
750-999	4	38.8	0	0.0	0	0.0	43	417.5
1000-1249	6	47.2	0	0.0	0	0.0	40	315.0
1250-1499	8	54.8	0	0.0	0	0.0	34	232.9
1500-1999	6	11.3	1	1.9	0	0.0	69	129.7
2000-2499	10	6.7	1	0.7	0	0.0	51	34.0
2500-2999	11	1.7	3	0.5	0	0.0	70	10.7
3000-3499	14	0.7	1	0.1	0	0.0	51	2.6
3500-3999	7	0.3	0	0.0	0	0.0	26	1.2
4000-4499	5	0.6	1	0.1	0	0.0	16	1.9
4500 and over	1	0.6	0	0.0	0	0.0	7	4.0
Not Stated	0	0.0	0	0.0	0	0.0	4	333.3
Total	79	1.3	7	0.1	0	0.0	483	8.0

* Note See Appendix D for a list of the International Classification of Disease codes corresponding to each cause of death.

Table 5.4
Age at Death
Early Neonatal Deaths, 2003

Singleton Births

Time		Frequency	Per Cent
Completed Hours	<1	35	22.4
	1	19	12.2
	2	9	5.8
	3	12	7.7
	4	3	1.9
	5	3	1.9
	6	2	1.3
	7	5	3.2
	8	1	0.6
	9	1	0.6
	10	1	0.6
	11	3	1.9
	12	1	0.6
	13	1	0.6
	16	1	0.6
	19	2	1.3
	20	3	1.9
	21	1	0.6
Total under 1 Day		**103**	**66.0**
Days	1	15	9.6
	2	13	8.3
	3	6	3.8
	4	4	2.6
	5	4	2.6
	6	2	1.3
Total under 1 Week		**44**	**28.2**
Unknown		9	5.8
Total		**156**	**100.0**

Table 5.5

**Percentage Distribution of Live Births
by Infant's Length of Stay in Hospital, 2003**

Singleton Births

Infant's Length of Stay (Days)	Live Births	Per Cent (%) Live Births
0-2	22,872	38.5
3-5	31,504	53.0
6-10	3,659	6.2
11-28	932	1.6
29 or more	378	0.6
Not Stated	100	0.2
Total	59,445	100.0

Note:
-This table does not include domiciliary births and early neonatal deaths.
-'Not Stated' includes 36 births where place of birth was recorded as domiciliary but birth was registered by a hospital. Mother and infant were not admitted under a planned community midwife scheme therefore infant's length of stay was not applicable.

Table 5.6

**Percentage of Stillbirths and Early Neonatal Deaths
Undergoing Post-Mortem Examinations, 2003**

Singleton Births

Post-Mortem	Type of Death		
Frequency Row Per Cent Col. Per Cent	Early Neonatal Deaths	Stillbirths	Total
Post-Mortem	62	156	218
	28.44	71.56	
	39.74	47.71	45.13
No Post-Mortem	81	166	247
	32.79	67.21	
	51.92	50.76	51.14
Not Stated	13	5	18
	72.22	27.78	
	8.33	1.53	3.73
Total	156	327	483
	32.30	67.70	100.00

Note: See Appendix F for an explanation of the table format.

Section 5
Perinatal Outcomes

Part 2 Multiple Births

Table 5.7
Live Births, Antepartum and Intrapartum Stillbirths, Early Neonatal Deaths
and Mortality Rates by Birthweight, 2003

Multiple Births

Birthweight (grams)	Live Births	Per Cent (%) Live Births	Ante-partum Stillbirths	Intra-partum Stillbirths	Not Stated	Stillbirth Rate	Early Neonatal Deaths	Early Neonatal Rate	Perinatal Mortality Rate	Adjusted PMR
500-749	22	1.2	3	2	4	290.3	15	681.8	774.2	758.6
750-999	24	1.3	3	0	3	200.0	4	166.7	333.3	333.3
1000-1249	30	1.7	3	0	1	117.6	0	0.0	117.6	117.6
1250-1499	53	3.0	0	0	0	0.0	0	0.0	0.0	0.0
1500-1999	215	12.0	0	1	1	9.2	1	4.7	13.8	9.3
2000-2499	465	25.9	2	1	0	6.4	1	2.2	8.5	8.5
2500-2999	607	33.8	3	0	0	4.9	0	0.0	4.9	4.9
3000-3499	335	18.7	0	0	0	0.0	0	0.0	0.0	0.0
3500-3999	43	2.4	1	0	0	22.7	0	0.0	22.7	22.7
4000-4499	1	0.1	0	0	0	0.0	0	0.0	0.0	0.0
Not Stated	0	0.0	2	0	0	1000.0	0	0.0	1000.0	1000.0
Total	**1,795**	**100.0**	**17**	**4**	**9**	**16.4**	**21**	**11.7**	**27.9**	**26.3**

Table 5.8

Stillbirths, Early Neonatal Deaths and Mortality Rates by Cause of Death, 2003

Multiple Births

Cause of Death	Stillbirths	Stillbirth Rate	Early Neonatal Deaths	Early Neonatal Rate	Total Deaths	Perinatal Mortality Rate
Other Central Nervous System Anomalies	0	0.0	1	0.6	1	0.6
Other Congenital Anomalies	0	0.0	1	0.6	1	0.6
Congenital Anomalies of Respiratory System	0	0.0	1	0.6	1	0.6
Other Maternal Complications	1	0.6	0	0.0	1	0.6
Other Placental Separation and Haemorrhage	6	3.3	3	1.7	9	4.9
Other Morphological and Functional Anomalies of Placenta	2	1.1	0	0.0	2	1.1
Other Complications of Placenta, Cord & Membrane	8	4.4	0	0.0	8	4.4
Other Complications of Labour/Delivery	0	0.0	2	1.1	2	1.1
Short Gestation and Low Birthweight	8	4.4	5	2.8	13	7.1
Birth Trauma	0	0.0	1	0.6	1	0.6
Intrauterine Hypoxia/Anoxia	1	0.6	0	0.0	1	0.6
Respiratory Distress Syndrome	0	0.0	5	2.8	5	2.7
Respiratory Conditions of Foetus/Newborn	0	0.0	2	1.1	2	1.1
Neonatal/Foetal Haemorrhage	1	0.6	0	0.0	1	0.6
Symptoms, Signs, and Ill-Defined Conditions	3	1.6	0	0.0	3	1.6
Total	**30**	**16.4**	**21**	**11.7**	**51**	**27.9**

Note: See Appendix D for a list of the International Classification of Diseases codes corresponding to each cause of death.

Table 5.9

Number of Perinatal Deaths by Birthweight and Cause of Death, 2003

Multiple Births

Birthweight (grams)	500-749	750-999	1000-1249	1500-1999	2000-2499	2500-2999	3500-3999	Not stated	Total
Other Central Nervous System Anomalies	1	0	0	0	0	0	0	0	1
Other Congenital Anomalies	1	0	0	1	0	0	0	0	2
Maternal Complications	0	0	1	0	0	0	0	0	1
Other Complications of Placenta, Cord & Membrane	7	4	2	1	2	2	1	0	19
Other Complications of Labour/Delivery	2	0	0	0	0	0	0	0	2
Slow Foetal Growth	8	3	1	0	0	0	0	1	13
Birth Trauma	1	0	0	0	0	0	0	0	1
Hypoxia/Anoxia	4	3	0	0	1	0	0	0	8
Neonatal/Foetal Haemorrhage	0	0	0	0	1	0	0	0	1
Symptoms, Signs, and Ill-Defined Conditions	0	0	0	1	0	1	0	1	3
Total	**24**	**10**	**4**	**3**	**4**	**3**	**1**	**2**	**51**

Note: See Appendix D for a list of the International Classification of Diseases codes corresponding to each cause of death.

Table 5.10
Age at Death
Early Neonatal Deaths, 2003

Multiple Births

Time		Frequency	Per Cent
Completed Hours	<1	1	4.8
	1	3	14.3
	2	3	14.3
	3	1	4.8
	4	2	9.5
	5	1	4.8
	6	1	4.8
	9	1	4.8
Total under 1 Day		**13**	**61.9**
Days	1	1	4.8
	2	4	19.0
	4	1	4.8
	5	1	4.8
Total under 1 Week		**7**	**33.3**
Unknown		**1**	**4.8**
Total		**21**	**100.0**

Table 5.11
Percentage Distribution of Live Births by Infant's Length of Stay in Hospital, 2003

Multiple Births

Length of Stay (Days)	Live Births	Per Cent (%) Live Births
0-2	100	5.6
3-5	801	45.2
6-10	437	24.6
11-28	296	16.7
29 or more	125	7.0
Not Stated	15	0.8
Total	**1,774**	**100.0**

Note:
-There were no domiciliary mulitple births.
-Early Neonatal Deaths are not included in this table.

Table 5.12

Percentage of Stillbirths and Early Neonatal Deaths Undergoing Post-Mortem Examinations, 2003

Multiple Births

Post-mortem Frequency Row Per Cent Col. Per Cent	Type of Death		
	Early Neonatal Deaths	Stillbirths	Total
Post-Mortem	6	13	19
	31.58	68.42	
	28.57	43.33	37.25
No Post-Mortem	14	17	31
	45.16	54.84	
	66.67	56.67	60.78
Not Stated	1	0	1
	100.00	0.00	
	4.76	0.00	1.96
Total	**21**	**30**	**51**
	41.18	**58.82**	**100.00**

Note: See Appendix F for an explanation of the table format.

Appendices

DEFINITIONS

This section collates the definitions of the terms used in the analyses for this report.

OUTCOMES AND RATES

Birth Rate: The Birth Rate or Crude Birth Rate is the ratio of total live births to total population over a specified period of time. The birth rate is often expressed as the number of live births per 1,000 of the population per year.

Live Birth (LB): A live birth is defined as the complete expulsion or extraction from its mother of a product of conception, irrespective of the duration of pregnancy, which, after such separation, breathes or shows any other evidence of life, such as beating of the heart, pulsation of the umbilical cord, or definite movement of voluntary muscles, whether or not the umbilical cord has been cut or the placenta is attached. In accordance with World Health Organisation (WHO) guidelines, live births weighing less than 500 grams are not included in the national statistics.

Stillbirth (SB) and Stillbirth Rate: Foetal death is defined as death prior to the complete expulsion or extraction from its mother of a product of conception, irrespective of the duration of the pregnancy. A foetal death is indicated by the fact that, after such separation, the foetus does not breathe or show any other evidence of life, such as beating of the heart, pulsation of the umbilical cord, or definite movement of voluntary muscles. Following WHO guidelines, a stillbirth, in this report, refers to the death of a foetus weighing at least 500 grams. The stillbirth rate is given as follows:

$$\frac{\text{Number of Stillbirths x 1,000}}{\text{Total Number of Live Births and Stillbirths}}$$

Early Neonatal Death (ENND) and Early Neonatal Mortality Rate: An early neonatal death refers to the death of a live born infant during the first week of life. The early neonatal mortality rate is calculated as follows:

$$\frac{\text{Number of Early Neonatal Deaths x 1,000}}{\text{Total Number of Live Births}}$$

Perinatal Death and Perinatal Mortality Rate (PMR): Perinatal deaths include stillbirths and early neonatal deaths. The perinatal mortality rate (PMR) is calculated as follows:

$$\frac{\text{Number of Stillbirths and Early Neonatal Deaths X 1,000}}{\text{Total Number of Live Births and Stillbirths}}$$

In this report a second perinatal mortality rate has been calculated excluding all stillbirths and early neonatal deaths due to congenital anomalies. This **adjusted rate (Adjusted PMR)** to some extent removes those perinatal events where death was unavoidable, but no attempt has been made to exclude only invariably fatal congenital anomalies.

Congenital Anomalies are physiological or structural abnormalities that develop at or before birth and are present at the time of birth.[4]

Twinning Rate: This is given by

$$\frac{\text{Number of Twin Maternities} \times 1{,}000}{\text{Total Number of Maternities}}$$

Twin maternities, which resulted in stillbirths, are included in the calculation of the twinning rate.

Note: In this report, where rates are based on very small numbers, they should be interpreted with caution and should not be used as estimates of the true population rates.

---

[4] Congenital anomalies are those diseases/conditions categorised in ICD-9, Chapter XIV, codes 740.0- 759.9.

OTHER ITEMS

The definitions given below relate to the principal classification variables contained in the main section of the report and refer only to those terms where explanation is considered necessary. The definitions are grouped according to the section in which they first appear.

General Characteristics

Born Before Arrival (BBA): Born before arrival indicates that an infant was delivered before arrival at hospital.

Domiciliary birth: Domiciliary births are *planned* home births. The vast majority of these are attended by an independent midwife and are not associated with a hospital. In 2003 there were 37 births under hospital administered home birth schemes. For the purposes of this report these births are treated as hospital births due to the small numbers.

Parity: Maternal parity indicates a mother's total number of previous live births and stillbirths.

Marital status: Five categories are recognised as specified below:

i.   Married.

ii.   Single or Never Married.

iii.   Widowed.

iv.   Separated: covers the following categories:
- Deserted.
- Legally separated.
- Church decree of nullity.
- Otherwise separated.

v.   Divorced.

Father's Occupation: Occupations are coded and grouped, with minor modifications, according to the CSO system of socio-economic groupings as used in the *1991 Census of Population*, Volume 6. Details are given in Appendix C.

Mother's Occupation: Occupations are coded and grouped, with minor modifications, according to the CSO system of socio-economic groupings as used in the *1991 Census of Population*, Volume 6. Details are given in Appendix C.

Birthweight: Birthweight is given in grams and hospitals are asked to record the weight within the first hour after birth. In accordance with WHO guidelines, infants weighing under 500 grams are not included in the national statistics.

Period of Gestation: Gestational age at delivery is recorded in completed weeks and is measured or estimated according to the best method available in each case.

Time since last birth: This variable gives the time, grouped into yearly intervals, since the mother's last live birth or stillbirth.

Perinatal care

Antenatal Length of Stay: This is computed as the difference, in days, between a mother's date of admission and her date of delivery. Domiciliary births are not included in tables relating to this variable.

Postnatal Length of Stay: This is computed as the difference, in days, between the date of delivery and the date of the mother's discharge from hospital. A return of 'not stated' for this variable may indicate that the completed form was returned before the mother had been discharged. Domiciliary births are not included in tables relating to this variable.

Immunity to Rubella: An affirmative answer should be recorded only where there is documented evidence of a rubella antibody test. A history of rubella or previous immunisation is not sufficient.

Method of delivery: Six categories are used:

i.   Spontaneous cephalic delivery, without any of the following:
ii.   Breech delivery, spontaneous, with or without forceps to after-coming head, breech extraction.
iii.   Forceps delivery.
iv.   Vacuum extraction.[5]
v.   Caesarean section.
vi.   Other specified and Combined (e.g combination of spontaneous delivery followed by a vacuum extraction or caesarean section).

Hospital Admission Booked or Unbooked: Indicates whether a mother's admission into hospital for delivery was booked or unbooked prior to delivery. Domiciliary births are not included in the tables relating to this variable.

Type of Feeding: Indicates whether artificial, breastfeeding or a combination of both was being used at the time of discharge. The **Breastfeeding Rate** is based on live births only (excluding ENNDs), and is calculated as follows;

$$\frac{\text{Number of Mother's Breastfeeding x 100}}{\text{Total Live Births}}$$

Transfer of Infants: This identifies infants who were transferred to another hospital for medical reasons.

Size of Maternity Unit: Size in this context refers to the number of perinatal events occurring during the year.

[5] Also known as Ventouse Deliveries (Source: Jane Henderson, Leslie L. Davidson, Jean Chapple, Jo Garcia, Stavros Petrou, "Pregnancy and Childbirth", Health Care Needs Assessment, http://hcna.radcliffe-oxford.com/pregframe.htm, date consulted 21st November 2006.)

Perinatal Outcomes

Antepartum and Intrapartum Stillbirths: These refer to stillbirths occurring prior to and during labour respectively.

Cause of Death: This categorisation indicates the principal underlying pathological cause, which in the opinion of the certifier made the greatest contribution to the death of the infant or foetus. In assigning cause of death, the guidelines recommended by the World Health Organisation have been followed. A summary of these guidelines, together with a list of the International Classification of Disease codes grouped into each category, is provided in Appendix D.

Age at Death: The age of early neonatal deaths is given in completed hours if the infant survived less than 1 day and in completed days otherwise.

Post-mortem: This indicates whether or not a post-mortem examination was performed. In some cases a return of 'not stated' may be due to the notification form being returned prior to post-mortem.

Length of Infant's Stay: This is computed as the difference, in days, between the infant's date of birth and the date of the infant's discharge from hospital. A return of 'not stated' for this variable may indicate that the completed form was returned before the infant had been discharged. Where an infant was transferred to another hospital, the date of the transfer is given as the date of the infant's discharge. Domiciliary births and perinatal deaths are not included in the tables relating to this variable.

Note:
- All perinatal statistics and definitions are based on WHO ICD-9 Classifications.
- Where a particular value of a variable does not occur in a table, the row corresponding to that value is not included. This arises most frequently in relation to multiple births. For example, in Table 3.15 the values for 'under 15' are not included as there are no occurrences of these multiple births for mother's age 'under 15'.

The following format was used for births recorded in 2003

NOTIFICATION OF BIRTH -

To: The National Perinatal Reporting System, Economic and Social Research Institute, 4 Burlington Road, Dublin 4

1

TYPE OF BIRTH (Live = 1, Still = 2)   2 ☐   PLACE OF BIRTH (Hospital = 1, BBA = 2, Domiciliary = 3)   3 ☐

NAME AND_____

ADDRESS OF_____

HOSPITAL NO.   4 ☐☐☐   CASE NO.   7 ☐☐☐☐☐☐☐
                                       Y Y Y Y

HOSPITAL _____

INFANT

DATE OF BIRTH   15 ☐☐ ☐☐ ☐☐☐☐
                D D M M Y Y Y Y

IF MULTIPLE BIRTH   ORDER OF BIRTH   No. ☐ 23   of ☐ 24

TIME OF BIRTH

SEX (Male = 1, Female = 2, Indeterminate = 3)   25 ☐

BIRTHWEIGHT   26 ☐☐☐☐ GRAMMES

PERIOD OF GESTATION   30 ☐☐ WEEKS

FATHER

COUNTY _____   32 ☐☐☐

OCCUPATION_____   35 ☐☐

DATE OF BIRTH   37 ☐☐ ☐☐ ☐☐☐☐
                D D M M Y Y Y Y

MOTHER

COUNTY_____   45 ☐☐☐

OCCUPATION_____   48 ☐☐

DATE OF BIRTH   50 ☐☐ ☐☐ ☐☐☐☐
                D D M M Y Y Y Y

MARITAL STATUS (Married = 1, Single = 2, Widowed = 3, Separated = 4, Divorced, = 5)   58 ☐

DATE OF PRESENT MARRIAGE   59 ☐☐ ☐☐ ☐☐☐☐
                            D D M M Y Y Y Y

DATE OF LAST BIRTH (live or still)   67 ☐☐ ☐☐ ☐☐☐☐
                                      D D M M Y Y Y Y

NO. OF PREVIOUS   LIVE BIRTHS   75 ☐☐

CHILDREN STILL LIVING   77 ☐☐

STILL BIRTHS   79 ☐☐

SPONTANEOUS ABORTIONS   81 ☐☐

PERINATAL DEATH

TYPE OF DEATH (Early Neonatal = 1, Stillbirth = 2)   83 ☐

WAS AUTOPSY PERFORMED (Yes = 1, No = 2)   84 ☐

AGE OF DEATH   85 ☐☐ DAYS   86 ☐☐☐ HOURS

PLACE OF DEATH _____   88 ☐☐☐

IF STILLBIRTH,   DID DEATH OCCUR BEFORE LABOUR (1) DURING LABOUR (2) NOT KNOWN (3)   91 ☐

CAUSE OF DEATH

MAIN DISEASE OR CONDITION IN FETUS OR INFANT_____   92 ☐☐☐☐

OTHER DISEASES OR CONDITIONS IN FETUS OR INFANT_____   96 ☐☐☐☐

MOTHER'S HEALTH

ANTE-NATAL CARE THIS PREGNANCY (Hospital / Obstetrician = 1, G.P. Only = 2, Combined = 3, None = 4)   100 ☐

DATE OF FIRST VISIT TO DOCTOR DURING PREGNANCY   101 ☐☐ ☐☐ ☐☐☐☐
                                                  D D M M Y Y Y Y

DATE OF FIRST VISIT TO HOSPITAL DURING PREGNANCY   109 ☐☐ ☐☐ ☐☐☐☐
                                                    D D M M Y Y Y Y

WAS MOTHER IMMUNE TO RUBELLA (Yes = 1, No = 2, Not Known = 3)   117 ☐

METHOD OF DELIVERY (Spontaneous = 1, Breech ± Forceps = 2, Forceps = 3, Vac. Extraction = 4, Caesarean Sec. = 5, Other = 6)   118 ☐

MAIN MATERNAL DISEASE OR CONDITION AFFECTING FETUS OR INFANT

_____   119 ☐☐☐☐

OTHER MATERNAL DISEASE OR CONDITION AFFECTING FETUS OR INFANT

_____   123 ☐☐☐☐

INFANT'S HEALTH

TYPE OF FEEDING (Artificial = 1, Breast = 2, Combined = 3)   127 ☐

WAS BCG ADMINISTERED (Yes = 1, No = 2)   128 ☐

MAIN DISEASE OR CONGENITAL MALFORMATION AFFECTING INFANT

_____   129 ☐☐☐☐

OTHER DISEASES OR CONGENITAL MALFORMATIONS AFFECTING INFANT

_____   133 ☐☐☐☐

HOSPITAL

WAS ADMISSION BOOKED (Yes = 1, No = 2)   137 ☐

DATE OF MOTHER'S ADMISSION   138 ☐☐ ☐☐ ☐☐☐☐
                              D D M M Y Y Y Y

DATE OF MOTHER'S DISCHARGE   146 ☐☐ ☐☐ ☐☐☐☐
                              D D M M Y Y Y Y

DATE OF INFANT'S DISCHARGE   154 ☐☐ ☐☐ ☐☐☐☐
                              D D M M Y Y Y Y

WAS INFANT TRANSFERRED TO OTHER HOSPITAL FOR MEDICAL REASONS (Yes = 1, No = 2)   162 ☐

IF 'YES', NAME OF HOSPITAL _____

_____   163 ☐☐☐

GENERAL PRACTITIONER ATTENDED BY MOTHER

SIGNATURE   DATE

The following format outlines the new form introduced in May 2003 and effective from January 1st 2004.

Notification of Birth - To: National Perinatal Reporting System, The Economic & Social Research Institute, 4 Burlington Rd. Dublin 4

TYPE OF BIRTH 1 ☐   PLACE OF BIRTH (Hospital = 1, BBA = 2, Domiciliary = 3)   2 ☐   NAME AND _____
(Live = 1, Still = 2)

ADDRESS OF _____

HOSPITAL NO. 3 ☐☐☐   CASE NO. 6 ☐☐☐☐☐☐☐ Y Y Y Y

HOSPITAL _____

INFANT'S DETAILS

DATE OF BIRTH (DD/MM/YYYY)   14 ☐☐☐☐☐☐☐☐

TIME OF BIRTH

IF MULTIPLE BIRTH   ORDER OF BIRTH   No. ☐ 22   of ☐ 23

SEX (Male = 1, Female = 2, Indeterminate = 3)   24 ☐

BIRTHWEIGHT   25 ☐☐☐☐ GRAMMES

PERIOD OF GESTATION   29 ☐☐ WEEKS

FATHER'S DETAILS

COUNTY _____ 31 ☐☐☐

COUNTRY _____ 34 ☐☐☐

NATIONALITY _____ 38 ☐☐☐

OCCUPATION _____ 42 ☐☐

DATE OF BIRTH (DDMMYYYY)   44 ☐☐☐☐☐☐☐☐

MOTHER'S DETAILS

COUNTY _____ 52 ☐☐☐

COUNTRY _____ 55 ☐☐☐

NATIONALITY _____ 59 ☐☐☐

OCCUPATION _____ 63 ☐☐

DATE OF BIRTH (DDMMYYYY)   65 ☐☐☐☐☐☐☐☐

MARITAL STATUS (Married = 1, Never Married = 2, Widowed = 3, Married but Separated = 4, Divorced, = 5) 73 ☐

DATE OF PRESENT MARRIAGE (DDMMYYYY)   74 ☐☐☐☐☐☐☐☐

DATE OF LAST BIRTH (live or still) (DDMMYYYY)   82 ☐☐☐☐☐☐☐☐

NO. OF PREVIOUS   LIVE BIRTHS   90 ☐☐

CHILDREN STILL LIVING   92 ☐☐

STILLBIRTHS   94 ☐☐

SPONTANEOUS ABORTIONS   96 ☐☐

PERINATAL DEATH

TYPE OF DEATH (Early Neonatal = 1, Stillbirth = 2)   98 ☐

WAS AUTOPSY PERFORMED (Yes = 1, No = 2)   99 ☐

AGE AT DEATH   100 ☐ DAYS   101 ☐☐ HOURS

PLACE OF DEATH _____ 103 ☐☐

IF STILLBIRTH,   DID DEATH OCCUR BEFORE LABOUR (1)
DURING LABOUR (2) NOT KNOWN (3)   106 ☐

CAUSE OF DEATH

MAIN DISEASE OR CONDITION IN FOETUS OR INFANT _____

_____ 107 ☐☐☐☐

OTHER DISEASES OR CONDITIONS IN FOETUS OR INFANT _____

_____ 112 ☐☐☐☐

Signature _____   Date _____

MOTHER'S HEALTH

ANTENATAL CARE THIS PREGNANCY
(Hospital / Obstetrician = 1, G.P. Only = 2, Combined = 3, None = 4, Midwife Only=5)   117 ☐

DATE OF FIRST VISIT TO DOCTOR
DURING PREGNANCY (DDMMYYYY)   118 ☐☐☐☐☐☐☐☐

DATE OF FIRST VISIT TO HOSPITAL
DURING PREGNANCY (DDMMYYYY)   126 ☐☐☐☐☐☐☐☐

WAS MOTHER IMMUNE TO RUBELLA
(Yes = 1, No = 2, Not Known = 3)   134 ☐

METHOD OF DELIVERY (Spontaneous = 1, Breech ± Forceps = 2,
Forceps = 3, Vac. Extraction = 4, Caesarean Sec. = 5, Other = 6)   135 ☐

MAIN MATERNAL DISEASE OR CONDITION AFFECTING FOETUS OR INFANT

_____ 136 ☐☐☐☐

OTHER MATERNAL DISEASES OR CONDITIONS AFFECTING FOETUS OR INFANT

_____ 141 ☐☐☐☐

INFANT'S HEALTH

TYPE OF FEEDING (Artificial = 1, Breast = 2, Combined = 3)   146 ☐

WAS BCG ADMINISTERED (Yes = 1, No = 2)   147 ☐

MAIN DISEASE OR CONGENITAL MALFORMATION AFFECTING INFANT

_____ 148 ☐☐☐☐

OTHER DISEASES OR CONGENITAL MALFORMATIONS AFFECTING INFANT

_____ 153 ☐☐☐☐

HOSPITAL

WAS ADMISSION BOOKED (Yes = 1, No = 2)   158 ☐

DATE OF MOTHER'S ADMISSION (DDMMYYYY)   159 ☐☐☐☐☐☐☐☐

DATE OF MOTHER'S DISCHARGE (DDMMYYYY)   167 ☐☐☐☐☐☐☐☐

DATE OF INFANT'S DISCHARGE (DDMMYYYY)   175 ☐☐☐☐☐☐☐☐

WAS INFANT TRANSFERRED TO OTHER HOSPITAL
FOR MEDICAL REASONS (Yes = 1, No = 2)   183 ☐

IF 'YES', NAME OF HOSPITAL _____

_____ 184 ☐☐

GENERAL PRACTITIONER ATTENDED BY MOTHER

BNF01/2003

Classification of Occupation

Occupations have been coded and classified into a set of socio-economic groups according to a system devised by the Central Statistics Office (CSO). The final CSO Category of 'Unknown' has been differentiated into 5 distinct groups for the purposes of the Perinatal Reporting System. These are 'Unemployed', 'Not Classifiable', 'Not Applicable', 'Home Duties' and 'Not Stated'. Occupation is coded as unemployed when occupation is given as unemployed and where no previous occupation is stated. If a previous occupation is stated then occupation is coded to the relevant category. 'Not Classifiable' has been used to categorise indecipherable, unclear, or unlisted occupations where efforts to clarify the information have failed. 'Home Duties' is entered where occupation has been entered as 'full-time mother/father/parent', 'stay at home mother/father/parent', 'housewife', 'home duties' etc. 'Not Stated' applies to those cases where either the mother's or father's occupation has been left blank or has been recorded as 'unknown'.

Under Father's occupation, the following applies:
'Not Applicable' is entered when the marital status of the mother has been given as single, widowed, separated or divorced and where father's occupation has been left blank. 'Not Stated' applies to those cases where the marital status of the mother is recorded as either married or not stated and where father's occupation has been left blank or has been recorded as 'unknown'. In either case, if an occupation is given for the father then the appropriate occupational code has been used.

The full list of socio-economic groups used in this report is given below:
* Farmers and Farm Managers
* Other Agricultural Occupations and Fishermen
* Higher Professional
* Lower Professional
* Employers and Managers
* Salaried Employees
* Intermediate Non-Manual Workers
* Other Non-Manual Workers
* Skilled Manual Workers
* Semi-Skilled Manual Workers
* Unskilled Manual Workers
* Unemployed
* Not Classifiable
* Not Applicable (Father's Occupation Only)
* Home Duties
* Not Stated

Cause of Death Classification

The main cause of death has been determined according to the guidelines set out by the World Health Organisation in the ninth revision of the International Classification of Diseases (ICD).[6] Briefly, the principal coding criteria are as follows:

1.   The main cause of death as far as possible should indicate the pathological condition of the infant or foetus, which in the opinion of the certifier made the greatest contribution towards the death.

2.   If heart or cardiac failure, asphyxia or anoxia (any condition in 768) or prematurity (any condition in 765) is entered as the main cause and other conditions of the infant or foetus are entered as secondary causes, then the first-mentioned of these other conditions is entered as the main cause of death.

3.   If two or more conditions are entered as the main cause of death then the first mentioned condition is coded as if it had been mentioned alone and the second-mentioned cause is coded as the secondary condition.

4.   If there is no entry for a main cause, then any secondary condition of the infant is coded as the main cause.

5.   If a maternal condition is entered in the section reserved for the infant's conditions or if an infant's condition is entered in the section provided for maternal conditions then the conditions are coded as if they had been entered in the respective correct section.

6.   If the foetus died before the onset of labour, then obstetrical complications that could not have affected the outcome are ignored as causes of death.

For the purpose of the cause of death tables included in this report, one further criterion has been applied. This is to the effect that where heart failure, asphyxia or anoxia (any condition in 768) or prematurity (any condition in 765) is coded as the main cause of death or where no infant's condition is given then, where a specific maternal condition is given, the main cause of death is classified under the maternal condition.

[6] World Health Organisation. 1978. *Manual of the International Classification of Diseases, Injuries and Causes of Death,* 9th Revision. Vol. 1. Geneva: WHO.

In Table 5.2, which contains a detailed classification of cause of death, the corresponding ICD numbers are listed in the left hand column of that table. For the less detailed tables (i.e., Tables 5.3, 5.8, and 5.9), the ICD codes relating to each cause of death category are given below:

ICD Codes	Cause of Death
740	Anencephalus and similar anomalies
741	Spina Bifida
742	Other congenital anomalies of the nervous system
745-747	Congenital anomalies of the heart
758	Chromosomal anomalies (including Down's Syndrome)
743-744, 748-757, 759	Other congenital anomalies
760-761	Maternal conditions and complications
762	Complications of the placenta, cord and membranes
763	Other complications of labour and delivery
764-765	Slow foetal growth, foetal malnutrition, and immaturity
766	Disorders relating to long gestation and high birthweight
767	Birth trauma
768-770	Intrauterine hypoxia and birth asphyxia and other respiratory conditions of foetus or newborn
771	Infections specific to the perinatal period
772	Foetal and neonatal haemorrhage
773	Haemolytic disease of foetus or newborn, due to iso-immunisation
775	Endocrine and metabolic disturbances specific to the foetus and newborn
778	Conditions involving the integument and temperature regulation of foetus and newborn
779.9	Maceration
780-799	Symptoms, signs and ill-defined conditions

All other codes have been classified to the category 'all other causes'. Where no cause has been given, perinatal deaths are categorised as 'cause not stated'.

Appendix E

Classification of County of Residence

The following codes are applied to mother's and father's county of residence. Where a Dublin postal code, such as Dublin 13, is entered then a code of 10 is applied for Dublin City. Where there is no postal code and Dublin is recorded then a code of 11 is applied for Dublin County. Where county of residence is recorded as Tipperary and North or South Riding is not specified, then the assignment of the code is based on the Health Board in which the birth occurred. For births occurring in the South-Eastern or Southern Health Boards where Tipperary is recorded as county of residence then a code of 62, Tipperary South Riding is applied. For births occurring in other Health Boards where Tipperary is recorded as county of residence then a code of 32, Tipperary North Riding is applied. Where a mother's or father's county of residence is unknown the code 99 is applied. The code 90 is applied where the address given is outside the Republic of Ireland.

Code	County
10	Dublin City
11	Dublin County
12	Kildare
13	Wicklow
20	Laois
21	Offaly
22	Longford
23	Westmeath
30	Clare
31	Limerick
32	Tipperary North Riding
40	Meath
41	Cavan
42	Monaghan
43	Louth
50	Donegal
51	Sligo
52	Leitrim
60	Carlow
61	Kilkenny
62	Tipperary South Riding
63	Waterford
64	Wexford
70	Cork
71	Kerry
80	Galway
81	Mayo
82	Roscommon
90	Other – all other places outside Republic of Ireland
99	Not Stated

Appendix F

Cross-Tabulations of Selected Variables: 2003

This appendix contains a range of cross-tabulations relating to live and still singleton births. A full list of these tables is given in the Table of Contents. The format of each cross-tabulation is identical. The values of the two variables are given along the top rows and left hand side column. The top number in each cell indicates the number of observations relating to that combination of variable values. The second number indicates the percentage contribution of that cell to the total for the whole row. The last number indicates the percentage contribution of that cell to the total for the whole column. The figures at the end of each row or column give the overall total for that row or column, and the associated percentages express each of these figures as a percentage of the grand total.

Table F1

Age of Mother by Maternal Parity, Live Births and Stillbirths, 2003

Singleton Births

Age of Mother Frequency Row Per Cent Col. Per Cent	Maternal Parity									
	0	1	2	3	4	5	6	More than 6	Not Stated	Total
Under 15 Years	15	0	0	0	0	0	0	0	0	15
	100.00	0.00	0.00	0.00	0.00	0.00	0.00	0.00	0.00	
	0.06	0.00	0.00	0.00	0.00	0.00	0.00	0.00	0.00	0.02
15-19 Years	2,525	262	31	3	0	0	0	1	0	2,822
	89.48	9.28	1.10	0.11	0.00	0.00	0.00	0.04	0.00	
	10.32	1.37	0.30	0.08	0.00	0.00	0.00	0.53	0.00	4.69
20-24 Years	5,119	2,418	642	153	23	3	0	2	1	8,361
	61.22	28.92	7.68	1.83	0.28	0.04	0.00	0.02	0.01	
	20.93	12.64	6.31	3.87	1.56	0.55	0.00	1.07	20.00	13.90
25-29 Years	6,729	4,875	1,840	650	219	75	31	7	1	14,427
	46.64	33.79	12.75	4.51	1.52	0.52	0.21	0.05	0.01	
	27.51	25.48	18.09	16.43	14.85	13.74	12.97	3.74	20.00	23.98
30-34 Years	7,239	7,395	3,895	1,289	468	163	58	47	1	20,555
	35.22	35.98	18.95	6.27	2.28	0.79	0.28	0.23	0.00	
	29.60	38.66	38.30	32.58	31.73	29.85	24.27	25.13	20.00	34.16
35-39 Years	2,403	3,597	3,225	1,496	557	215	107	65	2	11,667
	20.60	30.83	27.64	12.82	4.77	1.84	0.92	0.56	0.02	
	9.83	18.80	31.71	37.81	37.76	39.38	44.77	34.76	40.00	19.39
40-44 Years	393	546	519	357	195	88	36	57	0	2,191
	17.94	24.92	23.69	16.29	8.90	4.02	1.64	2.60	0.00	
	1.61	2.85	5.10	9.02	13.22	16.12	15.06	30.48	0.00	3.64
45 Years and over	7	15	12	8	9	2	6	7	0	66
	10.61	22.73	18.18	12.12	13.64	3.03	9.09	10.61	0.00	
	0.03	0.08	0.12	0.20	0.61	0.37	2.51	3.74	0.00	0.11
Not Stated	26	22	5	1	4	0	1	1	0	60
	43.33	36.67	8.33	1.67	6.67	0.00	1.67	1.67	0.00	
	0.11	0.12	0.05	0.03	0.27	0.00	0.42	0.53	0.00	0.10
Total	24,456	19,130	10,169	3,957	1,475	546	239	187	5	60,164
	40.65	31.80	16.90	6.58	2.45	0.91	0.40	0.31	0.01	100.00

Table F2
Method of Delivery by Maternal Parity, Live Births and Stillbirths, 2003

Singleton Births

Method of Delivery	Maternal Parity									
Frequency Row Per Cent Col. Per Cent	0	1	2	3	4	5	6	More than 6	Not Stated	Total
Spontaneous	11,800	13,269	7,481	3,016	1,153	426	184	143	3	37,475
	31.49	35.41	19.96	8.05	3.08	1.14	0.49	0.38	0.01	
	48.25	69.36	73.57	76.22	78.17	78.02	76.99	76.47	60.00	62.29
Breech/Forceps	149	58	25	15	8	1	1	1	0	258
	57.75	22.48	9.69	5.81	3.10	0.39	0.39	0.39	0.00	
	0.61	0.30	0.25	0.38	0.54	0.18	0.42	0.53	0.00	0.43
Forceps	1,393	238	85	14	3	3	1	0	0	1,737
	80.20	13.70	4.89	0.81	0.17	0.17	0.06	0.00	0.00	
	5.70	1.24	0.84	0.35	0.20	0.55	0.42	0.00	0.00	2.89
Vacuum Extraction	4,767	1,313	396	119	33	17	7	10	0	6,662
	71.56	19.71	5.94	1.79	0.50	0.26	0.11	0.15	0.00	
	19.49	6.86	3.89	3.01	2.24	3.11	2.93	5.35	0.00	11.07
Caesarean	6,290	4,208	2,158	782	272	98	46	33	1	13,888
	45.29	30.30	15.54	5.63	1.96	0.71	0.33	0.24	0.01	
	25.72	22.00	21.22	19.76	18.44	17.95	19.25	17.65	20.00	23.08
Other specified & Combined	53	41	24	10	6	1	0	0	0	135
	39.26	30.37	17.78	7.41	4.44	0.74	0.00	0.00	0.00	
	0.22	0.21	0.24	0.25	0.41	0.18	0.00	0.00	0.00	0.22
Not Stated	4	3	0	1	0	0	0	0	1	9
	44.44	33.33	0.00	11.11	0.00	0.00	0.00	0.00	11.11	
	0.02	0.02	0.00	0.03	0.00	0.00	0.00	0.00	20.00	0.01
Total	24,456	19,130	10,169	3,957	1,475	546	239	187	5	60,164
	40.65	31.80	16.90	6.58	2.45	0.91	0.40	0.31	0.01	100.00

Table F3

Marital Status by Age of Mother, Live Births and Stillbirths, 2003

Singleton Births

Marital Status	Age of Mother (Years)									
Frequency Row Per Cent Col. Per Cent	Under 15	15-19	20-24	25-29	30-34	35-39	40-44	45 and over	Not Stated	Total
Married	0	219	2,150	9,355	17,231	10,108	1,832	56	38	40,989
	0.00	0.53	5.25	22.82	42.04	24.66	4.47	0.14	0.09	
	0.00	7.76	25.71	64.84	83.83	86.64	83.61	84.85	63.33	68.13
Single	15	2,599	6,173	4,945	3,041	1,197	244	5	20	18,239
	0.08	14.25	33.85	27.11	16.67	6.56	1.34	0.03	0.11	
	100.00	92.10	73.83	34.28	14.79	10.26	11.14	7.58	33.33	30.32
Widowed	0	0	2	11	18	22	5	2	1	61
	0.00	0.00	3.28	18.03	29.51	36.07	8.20	3.28	1.64	
	0.00	0.00	0.02	0.08	0.09	0.19	0.23	3.03	1.67	0.10
Separated	0	4	32	99	210	250	73	3	0	671
	0.00	0.60	4.77	14.75	31.30	37.26	10.88	0.45	0.00	
	0.00	0.14	0.38	0.69	1.02	2.14	3.33	4.55	0.00	1.12
Divorced	0	0	3	15	54	89	37	0	0	198
	0.00	0.00	1.52	7.58	27.27	44.95	18.69	0.00	0.00	
	0.00	0.00	0.04	0.10	0.26	0.76	1.69	0.00	0.00	0.33
Not Stated	0	0	1	2	1	1	0	0	1	6
	0.00	0.00	16.67	33.33	16.67	16.67	0.00	0.00	16.67	
	0.00	0.00	0.01	0.01	0.00	0.01	0.00	0.00	1.67	0.01
Total	15	2,822	8,361	14,427	20,555	11,667	2,191	66	60	60,164
	0.02	4.69	13.90	23.98	34.16	19.39	3.64	0.11	0.10	100.00

Table F4

Marital Status by Age of Father, Live Births and Stillbirths, 2003

Singleton Births

Marital Status	Age of Father (Years)								
Frequency Row Per Cent Col. Per Cent	15-19	20-24	25-29	30-34	35-39	40-44	45 and over	Not Stated	Total
Married	61	689	4,576	13,464	10,758	3,815	1,017	6,609	40,989
	0.15	1.68	11.16	32.85	26.25	9.31	2.48	16.12	
	35.47	52.36	84.54	95.08	96.35	96.05	91.29	28.92	68.13
Single	111	616	798	631	355	133	80	15,515	18,239
	0.61	3.38	4.38	3.46	1.95	0.73	0.44	85.06	
	64.53	46.81	14.74	4.46	3.18	3.35	7.18	67.90	30.32
Widowed	0	0	3	6	3	2	2	45	61
	0.00	0.00	4.92	9.84	4.92	3.28	3.28	73.77	
	0.00	0.00	0.06	0.04	0.03	0.05	0.18	0.20	0.10
Separated	0	5	28	46	30	15	11	536	671
	0.00	0.75	4.17	6.86	4.47	2.24	1.64	79.88	
	0.00	0.38	0.52	0.32	0.27	0.38	0.99	2.35	1.12
Divorced	0	5	8	13	19	7	4	142	198
	0.00	2.53	4.04	6.57	9.60	3.54	2.02	71.72	
	0.00	0.38	0.15	0.09	0.17	0.18	0.36	0.62	0.33
Not Stated	0	1	0	0	1	0	0	4	6
	0.00	16.67	0.00	0.00	16.67	0.00	0.00	66.67	
	0.00	0.08	0.00	0.00	0.01	0.00	0.00	0.02	0.01
Total	172	1,316	5,413	14,160	11,166	3,972	1,114	22,851	60,164
	0.29	2.19	9.00	23.54	18.56	6.60	1.85	37.98	100.00

Table F5

Gestation Period at Delivery by Maternal Parity, Live Births and Stillbirths, 2003

Singleton Births

Gestation Period (weeks) Frequency Row Per Cent Col. Per Cent	Maternal Parity									
	0	1	2	3	4	5	6	More than 6	Not Stated	Total
Less than 22	3	0	0	0	0	0	0	0	0	3
	100.00	0.00	0.00	0.00	0.00	0.00	0.00	0.00	0.00	
	0.01	0.00	0.00	0.00	0.00	0.00	0.00	0.00	0.00	0.00
22-27	100	37	19	15	8	1	1	2	0	183
	54.64	20.22	10.38	8.20	4.37	0.55	0.55	1.09	0.00	
	0.41	0.19	0.19	0.38	0.54	0.18	0.42	1.07	0.00	0.30
28-31	200	58	26	29	10	0	3	3	0	329
	60.79	17.63	7.90	8.81	3.04	0.00	0.91	0.91	0.00	
	0.82	0.30	0.26	0.73	0.68	0.00	1.26	1.60	0.00	0.55
32-36	1,033	614	321	157	69	25	14	10	1	2,244
	46.03	27.36	14.30	7.00	3.07	1.11	0.62	0.45	0.04	
	4.22	3.21	3.16	3.97	4.68	4.58	5.86	5.35	20.00	3.73
37-41	21,473	17,599	9,426	3,565	1,333	490	207	163	4	54,260
	39.57	32.43	17.37	6.57	2.46	0.90	0.38	0.30	0.01	
	87.80	92.00	92.69	90.09	90.37	89.74	86.61	87.17	80.00	90.19
42 and over	1,641	820	372	191	55	30	13	9	0	3,131
	52.41	26.19	11.88	6.10	1.76	0.96	0.42	0.29	0.00	
	6.71	4.29	3.66	4.83	3.73	5.49	5.44	4.81	0.00	5.20
Not Stated	6	2	5	0	0	0	1	0	0	14
	42.86	14.29	35.71	0.00	0.00	0.00	7.14	0.00	0.00	
	0.02	0.01	0.05	0.00	0.00	0.00	0.42	0.00	0.00	0.02
Total	24,456	19,130	10,169	3,957	1,475	546	239	187	5	60,164
	40.65	31.80	16.90	6.58	2.45	0.91	0.40	0.31	0.01	100.00

Table F6

Age of Mother by Gestation Period at Delivery, Live Births and Stillbirths, 2003

Singleton Births

Age of Mother Frequency Row Per Cent Col. Per Cent	Gestation Period (weeks)							
	Less than 22	22-27	28-31	32-36	37-41	42 and over	Not Stated	Total
Under 15 Years	0	0	1	3	10	1	0	15
	0.00	0.00	6.67	20.00	66.67	6.67	0.00	
	0.00	0.00	0.30	0.13	0.02	0.03	0.00	0.02
15-19 Years	0	23	25	147	2,472	152	3	2,822
	0.00	0.82	0.89	5.21	87.60	5.39	0.11	
	0.00	12.57	7.60	6.55	4.56	4.85	21.43	4.69
20-24 Years	1	34	63	340	7,375	546	2	8,361
	0.01	0.41	0.75	4.07	88.21	6.53	0.02	
	33.33	18.58	19.15	15.15	13.59	17.44	14.29	13.90
25-29 Years	0	32	70	511	13,005	806	3	14,427
	0.00	0.22	0.49	3.54	90.14	5.59	0.02	
	0.00	17.49	21.28	22.77	23.97	25.74	21.43	23.98
30-34 Years	1	62	91	703	18,664	1,031	3	20,555
	0.00	0.30	0.44	3.42	90.80	5.02	0.01	
	33.33	33.88	27.66	31.33	34.40	32.93	21.43	34.16
35-39 Years	1	24	57	425	10,641	518	1	11,667
	0.01	0.21	0.49	3.64	91.21	4.44	0.01	
	33.33	13.11	17.33	18.94	19.61	16.54	7.14	19.39
40-44 Years	0	6	18	104	1,987	75	1	2,191
	0.00	0.27	0.82	4.75	90.69	3.42	0.05	
	0.00	3.28	5.47	4.63	3.66	2.40	7.14	3.64
45 Years and over	0	0	2	6	57	1	0	66
	0.00	0.00	3.03	9.09	86.36	1.52	0.00	
	0.00	0.00	0.61	0.27	0.11	0.03	0.00	0.11
Not Stated	0	2	2	5	49	1	1	60
	0.00	3.33	3.33	8.33	81.67	1.67	1.67	
	0.00	1.09	0.61	0.22	0.09	0.03	7.14	0.10
Total	3	183	329	2,244	54,260	3,131	14	60,164
	0.00	0.30	0.55	3.73	90.19	5.20	0.02	100.00

Table F7

Method of Delivery by Age of Mother, Live Births and Stillbirths, 2003

Singleton Births

Method of Delivery	Age of Mother (Years)									
Frequency Row Per Cent Col. Per Cent	Under 15	15-19	20-24	25-29	30-34	35-39	40-44	45 and over	Not Stated	Total
Spontaneous	12	1,966	5,802	9,147	12,180	7,042	1,254	31	41	37,475
	0.03	5.25	15.48	24.41	32.50	18.79	3.35	0.08	0.11	
	80.00	69.67	69.39	63.40	59.26	60.36	57.23	46.97	68.33	62.29
Breech/Forceps	0	19	38	57	94	41	8	0	1	258
	0.00	7.36	14.73	22.09	36.43	15.89	3.10	0.00	0.39	
	0.00	0.67	0.45	0.40	0.46	0.35	0.37	0.00	1.67	0.43
Forceps	0	91	199	434	657	305	51	0	0	1,737
	0.00	5.24	11.46	24.99	37.82	17.56	2.94	0.00	0.00	
	0.00	3.22	2.38	3.01	3.20	2.61	2.33	0.00	0.00	2.89
Vacuum Extraction	1	378	943	1,714	2,409	1,031	177	5	4	6,662
	0.02	5.67	14.15	25.73	36.16	15.48	2.66	0.08	0.06	
	6.67	13.39	11.28	11.88	11.72	8.84	8.08	7.58	6.67	11.07
Caesarean	2	364	1,368	3,044	5,166	3,211	691	30	12	13,888
	0.01	2.62	9.85	21.92	37.20	23.12	4.98	0.22	0.09	
	13.33	12.90	16.36	21.10	25.13	27.52	31.54	45.45	20.00	23.08
Other specified & Combined	0	4	11	28	47	36	9	0	0	135
	0.00	2.96	8.15	20.74	34.81	26.67	6.67	0.00	0.00	
	0.00	0.14	0.13	0.19	0.23	0.31	0.41	0.00	0.00	0.22
Not Stated	0	0	0	3	2	1	1	0	2	9
	0.00	0.00	0.00	33.33	22.22	11.11	11.11	0.00	22.22	
	0.00	0.00	0.00	0.02	0.01	0.01	0.05	0.00	3.33	0.01
Total	15	2,822	8,361	14,427	20,555	11,667	2,191	66	60	60,164
	0.02	4.69	13.90	23.98	34.16	19.39	3.64	0.11	0.10	100.00

Table F8

Birthweight by Gestation Period at Delivery, Live Births and Stillbirths, 2003

Singleton Births

Birthweight (grams) Frequency Row Per Cent Col. Per Cent	Gestation Period (weeks)							
	Less than 22	22-27	28-31	32-36	37-41	42 and over	Not Stated	Total
500-749	3	82	14	2	0	0	2	103
	2.91	79.61	13.59	1.94	0.00	0.00	1.94	
	100.00	44.81	4.26	0.09	0.00	0.00	14.29	0.17
750-999	0	53	44	6	0	0	0	103
	0.00	51.46	42.72	5.83	0.00	0.00	0.00	
	0.00	28.96	13.37	0.27	0.00	0.00	0.00	0.17
1000-1249	0	35	59	31	1	0	1	127
	0.00	27.56	46.46	24.41	0.79	0.00	0.79	
	0.00	19.13	17.93	1.38	0.00	0.00	7.14	0.21
1250-1499	0	6	74	59	6	0	1	146
	0.00	4.11	50.68	40.41	4.11	0.00	0.68	
	0.00	3.28	22.49	2.63	0.01	0.00	7.14	0.24
1500-1999	0	2	110	346	74	0	0	532
	0.00	0.38	20.68	65.04	13.91	0.00	0.00	
	0.00	1.09	33.43	15.42	0.14	0.00	0.00	0.88
2000-2499	0	2	20	632	840	6	1	1,501
	0.00	0.13	1.33	42.11	55.96	0.40	0.07	
	0.00	1.09	6.08	28.16	1.55	0.19	7.14	2.49
2500-2999	0	0	3	718	5,692	110	4	6,527
	0.00	0.00	0.05	11.00	87.21	1.69	0.06	
	0.00	0.00	0.91	32.00	10.49	3.51	28.57	10.85
3000-3499	0	0	1	331	18,804	741	1	19,878
	0.00	0.00	0.01	1.67	94.60	3.73	0.01	
	0.00	0.00	0.30	14.75	34.66	23.67	7.14	33.04
3500-3999	0	0	2	92	19,483	1,271	2	20,850
	0.00	0.00	0.01	0.44	93.44	6.10	0.01	
	0.00	0.00	0.61	4.10	35.91	40.59	14.29	34.66
4000-4499	0	0	0	22	7,821	803	1	8,647
	0.00	0.00	0.00	0.25	90.45	9.29	0.01	
	0.00	0.00	0.00	0.98	14.41	25.65	7.14	14.37
4500 and over	0	0	0	3	1,535	200	0	1,738
	0.00	0.00	0.00	0.17	88.32	11.51	0.00	
	0.00	0.00	0.00	0.13	2.83	6.39	0.00	2.89
Not Stated	0	3	2	2	4	0	1	12
	0.00	25.00	16.67	16.67	33.33	0.00	8.33	
	0.00	1.64	0.61	0.09	0.01	0.00	7.14	0.02
Total	3	183	329	2,244	54,260	3,131	14	60,164
	0.00	0.30	0.55	3.73	90.19	5.20	0.02	100.00

Table F9

Method of Delivery by Mother's Length of Stay in Hospital after Delivery, 2003

Singleton Births

Method of Delivery	Postnatal Length of Stay								
Frequency Row Per Cent Col. Per Cent	0-1 Days	2 Days	3-5 Days	6-8 Days	9-11 Days	12-14 Days	2 weeks or more	Not Stated	Total
Spontaneous	6,665	13,814	16,109	496	79	17	19	41	37,240
	17.90	37.09	43.26	1.33	0.21	0.05	0.05	0.11	
	90.63	85.42	49.36	15.40	22.70	22.08	27.94	78.85	62.14
Breech/Forceps	54	49	143	8	2	0	0	1	257
	21.01	19.07	55.64	3.11	0.78	0.00	0.00	0.39	
	0.73	0.30	0.44	0.25	0.57	0.00	0.00	1.92	0.43
Forceps	94	336	1,229	65	10	1	2	0	1,737
	5.41	19.34	70.75	3.74	0.58	0.06	0.12	0.00	
	1.28	2.08	3.77	2.02	2.87	1.30	2.94	0.00	2.90
Vacuum Extraction	481	1,737	4,245	165	27	4	3	0	6,662
	7.22	26.07	63.72	2.48	0.41	0.06	0.05	0.00	
	6.54	10.74	13.01	5.12	7.76	5.19	4.41	0.00	11.12
Caesarean	56	232	10,853	2,420	226	52	44	5	13,888
	0.40	1.67	78.15	17.43	1.63	0.37	0.32	0.04	
	0.76	1.43	33.25	75.13	64.94	67.53	64.71	9.62	23.17
Other specified & Combined	3	4	54	67	4	3	0	0	135
	2.22	2.96	40.00	49.63	2.96	2.22	0.00	0.00	
	0.04	0.02	0.17	2.08	1.15	3.90	0.00	0.00	0.23
Not Stated	1	0	3	0	0	0	0	5	9
	11.11	0.00	33.33	0.00	0.00	0.00	0.00	55.56	
	0.01	0.00	0.01	0.00	0.00	0.00	0.00	9.62	0.02
Total	7,354	16,172	32,636	3,221	348	77	68	52	59,928
	12.27	26.99	54.46	5.37	0.58	0.13	0.11	0.09	100.00

Note:
- 'Not Stated' includes 36 births where place of birth was recorded as domiciliary but birth was registered by hospital. Mother was not admitted under a planned community midwife scheme, therefore, dates of mother's length of stay were not applicable.
- Domiciliary births, of which there were 236, are excluded from this table. See Appendix H for detailed analysis.

Table F10

Maternal Parity by Mother's Length of Stay in Hospital after Delivery, Live Births and Stillbirths, 2003

Singleton Births

Maternal Parity Frequency Row Per Cent Col. Per Cent	Postnatal Length of Stay								
	0-1 Days	2 Days	3-5 Days	6-8 Days	9-11 Days	12-14 Days	2 weeks or more	Not Stated	Total
0	1,291	4,649	16,445	1,756	188	41	41	10	24,421
	5.29	19.04	67.34	7.19	0.77	0.17	0.17	0.04	
	17.56	28.75	50.39	54.52	54.02	53.25	60.29	19.23	40.75
1	2,921	6,155	9,063	781	78	15	17	15	19,045
	15.34	32.32	47.59	4.10	0.41	0.08	0.09	0.08	
	39.72	38.06	27.77	24.25	22.41	19.48	25.00	28.85	31.78
2	1,793	3,273	4,535	416	53	9	6	15	10,100
	17.75	32.41	44.90	4.12	0.52	0.09	0.06	0.15	
	24.38	20.24	13.90	12.92	15.23	11.69	8.82	28.85	16.85
3	788	1,321	1,624	159	19	9	2	5	3,927
	20.07	33.64	41.35	4.05	0.48	0.23	0.05	0.13	
	10.72	8.17	4.98	4.94	5.46	11.69	2.94	9.62	6.55
4	318	471	585	71	9	2	1	5	1,462
	21.75	32.22	40.01	4.86	0.62	0.14	0.07	0.34	
	4.32	2.91	1.79	2.20	2.59	2.60	1.47	9.62	2.44
5	123	170	229	19	0	0	1	0	542
	22.69	31.37	42.25	3.51	0.00	0.00	0.18	0.00	
	1.67	1.05	0.70	0.59	0.00	0.00	1.47	0.00	0.90
6	67	73	86	11	0	1	0	1	239
	28.03	30.54	35.98	4.60	0.00	0.42	0.00	0.42	
	0.91	0.45	0.26	0.34	0.00	1.30	0.00	1.92	0.40
More than 6	52	58	68	8	1	0	0	0	187
	27.81	31.02	36.36	4.28	0.53	0.00	0.00	0.00	
	0.71	0.36	0.21	0.25	0.29	0.00	0.00	0.00	0.31
Not Stated	1	2	1	0	0	0	0	1	5
	20.00	40.00	20.00	0.00	0.00	0.00	0.00	20.00	
	0.01	0.01	0.00	0.00	0.00	0.00	0.00	1.92	0.01
Total	7,354	16,172	32,636	3,221	348	77	68	52	59,928
	12.27	26.99	54.46	5.37	0.58	0.13	0.11	0.09	100.00

Note:
- 'Not Stated' includes 36 births where place of birth was recorded as domiciliary but birth was registered by a hospital. Mother was not admitted under a planned community midwife scheme, therefore, dates of mother's length of stay were not applicable.
- Domiciliary births, of which there were 236, are excluded from this table. See Appendix H for detailed analysis.

Table F11
Father's Occupation by Infant's Birthweight, Live Births and Stillbirths, 2003

Singleton Births

Father's Occupation	Birthweight (grams)												
Frequency Row Per Cent Col. Per Cent	500-749	750-999	1000-1249	1250-1499	1500-1999	2000-2499	2500-2999	3000-3499	3500-3999	4000-4499	4500 and over	Not Stated	Total
Farmers & Farm Managers	2	6	7	6	17	54	193	743	964	466	101	1	2,560
	0.08	0.23	0.27	0.23	0.66	2.11	7.54	29.02	37.66	18.20	3.95	0.04	
	1.94	5.83	5.51	4.11	3.20	3.60	2.96	3.74	4.62	5.39	5.81	8.33	4.26
Other Agricultural Occupations & Fishermen	1	0	2	1	4	12	53	171	214	95	27	0	580
	0.17	0.00	0.34	0.17	0.69	2.07	9.14	29.48	36.90	16.38	4.66	0.00	
	0.97	0.00	1.57	0.68	0.75	0.80	0.81	0.86	1.03	1.10	1.55	0.00	0.96
Higher- Professional	5	6	6	6	29	68	325	1,233	1,387	601	125	1	3,792
	0.13	0.16	0.16	0.16	0.76	1.79	8.57	32.52	36.58	15.85	3.30	0.03	
	4.85	5.83	4.72	4.11	5.45	4.53	4.98	6.20	6.65	6.95	7.19	8.33	6.30
Lower- Professional	3	1	4	4	22	54	255	924	1,134	520	86	0	3,007
	0.10	0.03	0.13	0.13	0.73	1.80	8.48	30.73	37.71	17.29	2.86	0.00	
	2.91	0.97	3.15	2.74	4.14	3.60	3.91	4.65	5.44	6.01	4.95	0.00	5.00
Managers	2	7	18	11	25	72	404	1,488	1,860	860	126	0	4,873
	0.04	0.14	0.37	0.23	0.51	1.48	8.29	30.54	38.17	17.65	2.59	0.00	
	1.94	6.80	14.17	7.53	4.70	4.80	6.19	7.49	8.92	9.95	7.25	0.00	8.10
Salaried- Employees	0	3	2	4	10	30	146	494	582	240	46	0	1,557
	0.00	0.19	0.13	0.26	0.64	1.93	9.38	31.73	37.38	15.41	2.95	0.00	
	0.00	2.91	1.57	2.74	1.88	2.00	2.24	2.49	2.79	2.78	2.65	0.00	2.59
Non-Manual Workers	5	5	5	5	26	92	400	1,356	1,511	686	144	2	4,237
	0.12	0.12	0.12	0.12	0.61	2.17	9.44	32.00	35.66	16.19	3.40	0.05	
	4.85	4.85	3.94	3.42	4.89	6.13	6.13	6.82	7.25	7.93	8.29	16.67	7.04
Other Non- Manual Workers	5	5	9	10	53	104	532	1,564	1,666	665	164	0	4,777
	0.10	0.10	0.19	0.21	1.11	2.18	11.14	32.74	34.88	13.92	3.43	0.00	
	4.85	4.85	7.09	6.85	9.96	6.93	8.15	7.87	7.99	7.69	9.44	0.00	7.94
Skilled Manual Workers	15	11	15	22	86	252	1,053	3,452	4,035	1,676	373	2	10,992
	0.14	0.10	0.14	0.20	0.78	2.29	9.58	31.40	36.71	15.25	3.39	0.02	
	14.56	10.68	11.81	15.07	16.17	16.79	16.13	17.37	19.35	19.38	21.46	16.67	18.27
Semi-skilled Manual Workers	3	3	4	2	18	65	276	853	932	372	71	1	2,600
	0.12	0.12	0.15	0.08	0.69	2.50	10.62	32.81	35.85	14.31	2.73	0.04	
	2.91	2.91	3.15	1.37	3.38	4.33	4.23	4.29	4.47	4.30	4.09	8.33	4.32
Unskilled Manual Workers	1	2	2	4	3	14	74	186	192	66	11	0	555
	0.18	0.36	0.36	0.72	0.54	2.52	13.33	33.51	34.59	11.89	1.98	0.00	
	0.97	1.94	1.57	2.74	0.56	0.93	1.13	0.94	0.92	0.76	0.63	0.00	0.92
Unemployed	2	11	6	10	24	58	315	758	651	243	63	1	2,142
	0.09	0.51	0.28	0.47	1.12	2.71	14.71	35.39	30.39	11.34	2.94	0.05	
	1.94	10.68	4.72	6.85	4.51	3.86	4.83	3.81	3.12	2.81	3.62	8.33	3.56
Not Classifiable	2	3	3	3	6	26	103	376	304	129	27	0	982
	0.20	0.31	0.31	0.31	0.61	2.65	10.49	38.29	30.96	13.14	2.75	0.00	
	1.94	2.91	2.36	2.05	1.13	1.73	1.58	1.89	1.46	1.49	1.55	0.00	1.63
Not Applicable	51	38	39	53	196	559	2,213	5,716	4,954	1,859	337	4	16,019
	0.32	0.24	0.24	0.33	1.22	3.49	13.81	35.68	30.93	11.60	2.10	0.02	
	49.51	36.89	30.71	36.30	36.84	37.24	33.91	28.76	23.76	21.50	19.39	33.33	26.63
Not Stated	6	2	5	5	13	41	185	564	464	169	37	0	1,491
	0.40	0.13	0.34	0.34	0.87	2.75	12.41	37.83	31.12	11.33	2.48	0.00	
	5.83	1.94	3.94	3.42	2.44	2.73	2.83	2.84	2.23	1.95	2.13	0.00	2.48
Total	103	103	127	146	532	1,501	6,527	19,878	20,850	8,647	1,738	12	60,164
	0.17	0.17	0.21	0.24	0.88	2.49	10.85	33.04	34.66	14.37	2.89	0.02	100.00

Note: In this table 'Not Classifiable' includes 89 Fathers whose occupation was recorded as 'Home Duties'.

Table F12
Mother's Occupation by Infant's Birthweight, Live Births and Stillbirths, 2003

Singleton Births

Mother's Occupation Frequency Row Per Cent Col. Per Cent	Birthweight (grams)												
	500-749	750-999	1000-1249	1250-1499	1500-1999	2000-2499	2500-2999	3000-3499	3500-3999	4000-4499	4500 and over	Not Stated	Total
Farmers & Farm Managers	0	2	0	0	2	0	13	27	42	17	3	0	106
	0.00	1.89	0.00	0.00	1.89	0.00	12.26	25.47	39.62	16.04	2.83	0.00	
	0.00	1.94	0.00	0.00	0.38	0.00	0.20	0.14	0.20	0.20	0.17	0.00	0.18
Other Agricultural Occupations & Fishermen	1	0	0	0	0	4	14	47	48	23	1	0	138
	0.72	0.00	0.00	0.00	0.00	2.90	10.14	34.06	34.78	16.67	0.72	0.00	
	0.97	0.00	0.00	0.00	0.00	0.27	0.21	0.24	0.23	0.27	0.06	0.00	0.23
Higher-Professional	7	3	2	1	17	36	211	861	1,031	447	67	1	2,684
	0.26	0.11	0.07	0.04	0.63	1.34	7.86	32.08	38.41	16.65	2.50	0.04	
	6.80	2.91	1.57	0.68	3.20	2.40	3.23	4.33	4.94	5.17	3.86	8.33	4.46
Lower-Professional	10	3	10	13	38	133	620	2,312	2,826	1,281	233	1	7,480
	0.13	0.04	0.13	0.17	0.51	1.78	8.29	30.91	37.78	17.13	3.11	0.01	
	9.71	2.91	7.87	8.90	7.14	8.86	9.50	11.63	13.55	14.81	13.41	8.33	12.43
Managers	4	4	12	7	32	81	301	1,090	1,377	596	119	0	3,623
	0.11	0.11	0.33	0.19	0.88	2.24	8.31	30.09	38.01	16.45	3.28	0.00	
	3.88	3.88	9.45	4.79	6.02	5.40	4.61	5.48	6.60	6.89	6.85	0.00	6.02
Salaried-Employees	0	2	5	2	7	22	85	303	335	148	22	0	931
	0.00	0.21	0.54	0.21	0.75	2.36	9.13	32.55	35.98	15.90	2.36	0.00	
	0.00	1.94	3.94	1.37	1.32	1.47	1.30	1.52	1.61	1.71	1.27	0.00	1.55
Non-Manual Workers	21	22	28	37	128	301	1,324	4,358	4,723	1,989	409	3	13,343
	0.16	0.16	0.21	0.28	0.96	2.26	9.92	32.66	35.40	14.91	3.07	0.02	
	20.39	21.36	22.05	25.34	24.06	20.05	20.28	21.92	22.65	23.00	23.53	25.00	22.18
Other Non-Manual Workers	12	8	8	14	40	174	729	2,099	2,025	834	152	1	6,096
	0.20	0.13	0.13	0.23	0.66	2.85	11.96	34.43	33.22	13.68	2.49	0.02	
	11.65	7.77	6.30	9.59	7.52	11.59	11.17	10.56	9.71	9.64	8.75	8.33	10.13
Skilled Manual Workers	0	0	1	0	2	21	65	210	242	105	20	0	666
	0.00	0.00	0.15	0.00	0.30	3.15	9.76	31.53	36.34	15.77	3.00	0.00	
	0.00	0.00	0.79	0.00	0.38	1.40	1.00	1.06	1.16	1.21	1.15	0.00	1.11
Semi-skilled Manual Workers	6	9	4	12	21	80	351	935	899	365	75	0	2,757
	0.22	0.33	0.15	0.44	0.76	2.90	12.73	33.91	32.61	13.24	2.72	0.00	
	5.83	8.74	3.15	8.22	3.95	5.33	5.38	4.70	4.31	4.22	4.32	0.00	4.58
Unskilled Manual Workers	0	0	0	0	0	0	2	4	2	0	0	0	8
	0.00	0.00	0.00	0.00	0.00	0.00	25.00	50.00	25.00	0.00	0.00	0.00	
	0.00	0.00	0.00	0.00	0.00	0.00	0.03	0.02	0.01	0.00	0.00	0.00	0.01
Unemployed	10	8	7	12	35	91	492	1,064	809	251	47	1	2,827
	0.35	0.28	0.25	0.42	1.24	3.22	17.40	37.64	28.62	8.88	1.66	0.04	
	9.71	7.77	5.51	8.22	6.58	6.06	7.54	5.35	3.88	2.90	2.70	8.33	4.70
Not Classifiable	4	7	9	7	21	67	265	773	689	254	35	0	2,131
	0.19	0.33	0.42	0.33	0.99	3.14	12.44	36.27	32.33	11.92	1.64	0.00	
	3.88	6.80	7.09	4.79	3.95	4.46	4.06	3.89	3.30	2.94	2.01	0.00	3.54
Home Duties	22	29	37	36	174	467	1,927	5,433	5,517	2,240	531	2	16,415
	0.13	0.18	0.23	0.22	1.06	2.84	11.74	33.10	33.61	13.65	3.23	0.01	
	21.36	28.16	29.13	24.66	32.71	31.11	29.52	27.33	26.46	25.90	30.55	16.67	27.28
Not Stated	6	6	4	5	15	24	128	362	285	97	24	3	959
	0.63	0.63	0.42	0.52	1.56	2.50	13.35	37.75	29.72	10.11	2.50	0.31	
	5.83	5.83	3.15	3.42	2.82	1.60	1.96	1.82	1.37	1.12	1.38	25.00	1.59
Total	103	103	127	146	532	1,501	6,527	19,878	20,850	8,647	1,738	12	60,164
	0.17	0.17	0.21	0.24	0.88	2.49	10.85	33.04	34.66	14.37	2.89	0.02	100.00

Note: 'Not Applicable' is not used in the classification of maternal occupation. See Appendix C for a description of the classification system for occupations.

Table F13
Father's Occupation by Interval in Years Since Last Birth, Live Births and Stillbirths, 2003

Singleton Births

Father's Occupation Frequency Row Per Cent Col. Per Cent	Interval Since Last Birth										Total
	No Previous Births	1 year or less	>1 year to 2 years	> 2 years to 3 years	> 3 years to 4 years	> 4 years to 5 years	> 5 years to 6 years	More than 6 years	No. of Previous Births Unknown	Not Stated	
Farmers & Farm Managers	703	27	539	546	258	173	93	183	0	38	2,560
	27.46	1.05	21.05	21.33	10.08	6.76	3.63	7.15	0.00	1.48	
	2.87	4.80	6.21	6.09	4.54	4.85	3.99	3.45	0.00	6.17	4.26
Other Agricultural Occupations & Fishermen	190	4	88	113	65	35	21	58	0	6	580
	32.76	0.69	15.17	19.48	11.21	6.03	3.62	10.00	0.00	1.03	
	0.78	0.71	1.01	1.26	1.14	0.98	0.90	1.09	0.00	0.97	0.96
Higher- Professional	1,442	24	708	757	376	176	99	180	0	30	3,792
	38.03	0.63	18.67	19.96	9.92	4.64	2.61	4.75	0.00	0.79	
	5.90	4.27	8.16	8.44	6.62	4.93	4.25	3.40	0.00	4.87	6.30
Lower- Professional	1,243	16	483	553	276	148	81	183	0	24	3,007
	41.34	0.53	16.06	18.39	9.18	4.92	2.69	6.09	0.00	0.80	
	5.08	2.85	5.57	6.16	4.86	4.15	3.48	3.45	0.00	3.90	5.00
Managers	1,783	35	752	938	549	307	171	303	0	35	4,873
	36.59	0.72	15.43	19.25	11.27	6.30	3.51	6.22	0.00	0.72	
	7.29	6.23	8.67	10.45	9.66	8.60	7.35	5.72	0.00	5.68	8.10
Salaried- Employees	589	8	246	270	176	104	59	93	0	12	1,557
	37.83	0.51	15.80	17.34	11.30	6.68	3.79	5.97	0.00	0.77	
	2.41	1.42	2.84	3.01	3.10	2.91	2.53	1.75	0.00	1.95	2.59
Non-Manual Workers	1,563	31	651	702	484	273	173	312	0	48	4,237
	36.89	0.73	15.36	16.57	11.42	6.44	4.08	7.36	0.00	1.13	
	6.39	5.52	7.50	7.82	8.52	7.65	7.43	5.89	0.00	7.79	7.04
Other Non- Manual Workers	1,653	40	664	759	519	332	225	541	0	44	4,777
	34.60	0.84	13.90	15.89	10.86	6.95	4.71	11.33	0.00	0.92	
	6.76	7.12	7.65	8.46	9.14	9.30	9.66	10.21	0.00	7.14	7.94
Skilled Manual Workers	3,836	102	1,625	1,862	1,228	727	458	1,024	1	129	10,992
	34.90	0.93	14.78	16.94	11.17	6.61	4.17	9.32	0.01	1.17	
	15.69	18.15	18.73	20.75	21.62	20.36	19.67	19.32	50.00	20.94	18.27
Semi-skilled Manual Workers	903	23	309	384	301	211	126	302	0	41	2,600
	34.73	0.88	11.88	14.77	11.58	8.12	4.85	11.62	0.00	1.58	
	3.69	4.09	3.56	4.28	5.30	5.91	5.41	5.70	0.00	6.66	4.32
Unskilled Manual Workers	153	9	97	75	69	34	31	80	0	7	555
	27.57	1.62	17.48	13.51	12.43	6.13	5.59	14.41	0.00	1.26	
	0.63	1.60	1.12	0.84	1.21	0.95	1.33	1.51	0.00	1.14	0.92
Unemployed	561	51	566	349	195	118	83	180	0	39	2,142
	26.19	2.38	26.42	16.29	9.10	5.51	3.87	8.40	0.00	1.82	
	2.29	9.07	6.52	3.89	3.43	3.31	3.57	3.40	0.00	6.33	3.56
Not Classifiable	387	10	195	147	75	59	32	74	0	3	982
	39.41	1.02	19.86	14.97	7.64	6.01	3.26	7.54	0.00	0.31	
	1.58	1.78	2.25	1.64	1.32	1.65	1.37	1.40	0.00	0.49	1.63
Not Applicable	8,971	161	1,444	1,279	981	790	628	1,637	1	127	16,019
	56.00	1.01	9.01	7.98	6.12	4.93	3.92	10.22	0.01	0.79	
	36.68	28.65	16.64	14.26	17.27	22.13	26.98	30.89	50.00	20.62	26.63
Not Stated	479	21	310	238	129	83	48	150	0	33	1,491
	32.13	1.41	20.79	15.96	8.65	5.57	3.22	10.06	0.00	2.21	
	1.96	3.74	3.57	2.65	2.27	2.32	2.06	2.83	0.00	5.36	2.48
Total	24,456	562	8,677	8,972	5,681	3,570	2,328	5,300	2	616	60,164
	40.65	0.93	14.42	14.91	9.44	5.93	3.87	8.81	0.00	1.02	100.00

Note: In this table 'Not Classifiable' includes 89 Fathers whose occupation was recorded as 'Home Duties'.

Table F14

Mother's Occupation by Interval in Years Since Last Birth, Live Births and Stillbirths, 2003

Singleton Births

Mother's Occupation — Frequency Row Per Cent Col. Per Cent	No Previous Births	1 year or less	>1 year to 2 years	> 2 years to 3 years	> 3 years to 4 years	> 4 years to 5 years	> 5 years to 6 years	More than 6 years	No. of Previous Births Unknown	Not Stated	Total
Farmers & Farm Managers	37	1	24	20	12	4	2	3	0	3	106
	34.91	0.94	22.64	18.87	11.32	3.77	1.89	2.83	0.00	2.83	
	0.15	0.18	0.28	0.22	0.21	0.11	0.09	0.06	0.00	0.49	0.18
Other Agricultural Occupations & Fishermen	78	0	18	15	5	6	3	12	0	1	138
	56.52	0.00	13.04	10.87	3.62	4.35	2.17	8.70	0.00	0.72	
	0.32	0.00	0.21	0.17	0.09	0.17	0.13	0.23	0.00	0.16	0.23
Higher-Professional	1,243	15	467	447	222	106	59	103	0	22	2,684
	46.31	0.56	17.40	16.65	8.27	3.95	2.20	3.84	0.00	0.82	
	5.08	2.67	5.38	4.98	3.91	2.97	2.53	1.94	0.00	3.57	4.46
Lower-Professional	3,134	31	1,292	1,315	643	372	215	416	0	62	7,480
	41.90	0.41	17.27	17.58	8.60	4.97	2.87	5.56	0.00	0.83	
	12.81	5.52	14.89	14.66	11.32	10.42	9.24	7.85	0.00	10.06	12.43
Managers	1,929	21	408	466	296	148	108	236	0	11	3,623
	53.24	0.58	11.26	12.86	8.17	4.09	2.98	6.51	0.00	0.30	
	7.89	3.74	4.70	5.19	5.21	4.15	4.64	4.45	0.00	1.79	6.02
Salaried-Employees	542	5	104	95	68	36	23	49	0	9	931
	58.22	0.54	11.17	10.20	7.30	3.87	2.47	5.26	0.00	0.97	
	2.22	0.89	1.20	1.06	1.20	1.01	0.99	0.92	0.00	1.46	1.55
Non-Manual Workers	6,413	102	1,392	1,735	1,221	755	490	1,134	1	100	13,343
	48.06	0.76	10.43	13.00	9.15	5.66	3.67	8.50	0.01	0.75	
	26.22	18.15	16.04	19.34	21.49	21.15	21.05	21.40	50.00	16.23	22.18
Other Non-Manual Workers	2,926	52	580	669	488	358	283	697	0	43	6,096
	48.00	0.85	9.51	10.97	8.01	5.87	4.64	11.43	0.00	0.71	
	11.96	9.25	6.68	7.46	8.59	10.03	12.16	13.15	0.00	6.98	10.13
Skilled Manual Workers	331	1	82	99	47	31	18	50	0	7	666
	49.70	0.15	12.31	14.86	7.06	4.65	2.70	7.51	0.00	1.05	
	1.35	0.18	0.95	1.10	0.83	0.87	0.77	0.94	0.00	1.14	1.11
Semi-skilled Manual Workers	1,313	10	249	299	231	165	126	335	0	29	2,757
	47.62	0.36	9.03	10.85	8.38	5.98	4.57	12.15	0.00	1.05	
	5.37	1.78	2.87	3.33	4.07	4.62	5.41	6.32	0.00	4.71	4.58
Unskilled Manual Workers	1	0	0	3	0	1	0	3	0	0	8
	12.50	0.00	0.00	37.50	0.00	12.50	0.00	37.50	0.00	0.00	
	0.00	0.00	0.00	0.03	0.00	0.03	0.00	0.06	0.00	0.00	0.01
Unemployed	1,317	42	460	311	197	112	104	231	0	53	2,827
	46.59	1.49	16.27	11.00	6.97	3.96	3.68	8.17	0.00	1.87	
	5.39	7.47	5.30	3.47	3.47	3.14	4.47	4.36	0.00	8.60	4.70
Not Classifiable	1,559	12	139	141	77	56	39	95	1	12	2,131
	73.16	0.56	6.52	6.62	3.61	2.63	1.83	4.46	0.05	0.56	
	6.37	2.14	1.60	1.57	1.36	1.57	1.68	1.79	50.00	1.95	3.54
Home Duties	3,172	255	3,314	3,242	2,122	1,387	824	1,864	0	235	16,415
	19.32	1.55	20.19	19.75	12.93	8.45	5.02	11.36	0.00	1.43	
	12.97	45.37	38.19	36.13	37.35	38.85	35.40	35.17	0.00	38.15	27.28
Not Stated	461	15	148	115	52	33	34	72	0	29	959
	48.07	1.56	15.43	11.99	5.42	3.44	3.55	7.51	0.00	3.02	
	1.89	2.67	1.71	1.28	0.92	0.92	1.46	1.36	0.00	4.71	1.59
Total	**24,456**	**562**	**8,677**	**8,972**	**5,681**	**3,570**	**2,328**	**5,300**	**2**	**616**	**60,164**
	40.65	**0.93**	**14.42**	**14.91**	**9.44**	**5.93**	**3.87**	**8.81**	**0.00**	**1.02**	**100.00**

Note: 'Not Applicable' is not used in the classification of maternal occupation. See Appendix C for a description of the classification system for occupations.

Table F15

Father's Occupation by Infant's Type of Feeding, Live Births Only, 2003

Singleton Births

Father's Occupation	Type of Feeding				
Frequency Row Per Cent Col. Per Cent	Artificial	Breast	Combined	Not Stated	Total
Farmers & Farm Managers	1,427	1,064	53	3	2,547
	56.03	41.77	2.08	0.12	
	4.33	4.29	2.63	3.45	4.26
Other Agricultural Occupations & Fishermen	340	232	7	0	579
	58.72	40.07	1.21	0.00	
	1.03	0.94	0.35	0.00	0.97
Higher-Professional	1,170	2,405	203	2	3,780
	30.95	63.62	5.37	0.05	
	3.55	9.70	10.07	2.30	6.32
Lower-Professional	975	1,905	114	1	2,995
	32.55	63.61	3.81	0.03	
	2.96	7.68	5.66	1.15	5.01
Managers	2,189	2,476	179	6	4,850
	45.13	51.05	3.69	0.12	
	6.64	9.99	8.88	6.90	8.11
Salaried-Employees	768	729	44	1	1,542
	49.81	47.28	2.85	0.06	
	2.33	2.94	2.18	1.15	2.58
Non-Manual Workers	2,059	2,003	156	4	4,222
	48.77	47.44	3.69	0.09	
	6.25	8.08	7.74	4.60	7.06
Other Non-Manual Workers	2,743	1,844	162	7	4,756
	57.67	38.77	3.41	0.15	
	8.33	7.44	8.04	8.05	7.95
Skilled Manual Workers	6,199	4,450	280	20	10,949
	56.62	40.64	2.56	0.18	
	18.82	17.95	13.90	22.99	18.30
Semi-skilled Manual Workers	1,740	780	69	0	2,589
	67.21	30.13	2.67	0.00	
	5.28	3.15	3.42	0.00	4.33
Unskilled Manual Workers	427	109	13	0	549
	77.78	19.85	2.37	0.00	
	1.30	0.44	0.65	0.00	0.92
Unemployed	1,184	806	132	7	2,129
	55.61	37.86	6.20	0.33	
	3.59	3.25	6.55	8.05	3.56
Not Classifiable	375	529	69	3	976
	38.42	54.20	7.07	0.31	
	1.14	2.13	3.42	3.45	1.63
Not Applicable	10,849	4,670	357	32	15,908
	68.20	29.36	2.24	0.20	
	32.93	18.84	17.72	36.78	26.59
Not Stated	500	788	177	1	1,466
	34.11	53.75	12.07	0.07	
	1.52	3.18	8.78	1.15	2.45
Total	32,945	24,790	2,015	87	59,837
	55.06	41.43	3.37	0.15	100.00

Note:
- In this table 'Not Classifiable' includes 89 fathers whose occupation was recorded as 'Home Duties'.
- 'Not Stated' contains 73 Early Neonatal Deaths for which Type of Feeding was not stated.

Table F16

Mother's Occupation by Infant's Type of Feeding, Live Births Only, 2003

Singleton Births

Mother's Occupation	Type of Feeding				
Frequency Row Per Cent Col. Per Cent	Artificial	Breast	Combined	Not Stated	Total
Farmers & Farm Managers	54	47	3	0	104
	51.92	45.19	2.88	0.00	
	0.16	0.19	0.15	0.00	0.17
Other Agricultural Occupations & Fishermen	54	80	4	0	138
	39.13	57.97	2.90	0.00	
	0.16	0.32	0.20	0.00	0.23
Higher-Professional	753	1,793	127	4	2,677
	28.13	66.98	4.74	0.15	
	2.29	7.23	6.30	4.60	4.47
Lower-Professional	2,502	4,676	261	8	7,447
	33.60	62.79	3.50	0.11	
	7.59	18.86	12.95	9.20	12.45
Managers	1,642	1,829	130	10	3,611
	45.47	50.65	3.60	0.28	
	4.98	7.38	6.45	11.49	6.03
Salaried-Employees	476	424	23	1	924
	51.52	45.89	2.49	0.11	
	1.44	1.71	1.14	1.15	1.54
Non-Manual Workers	8,278	4,681	321	17	13,297
	62.25	35.20	2.41	0.13	
	25.13	18.88	15.93	19.54	22.22
Other Non-Manual Workers	3,715	2,178	165	8	6,066
	61.24	35.91	2.72	0.13	
	11.28	8.79	8.19	9.20	10.14
Skilled Manual Workers	301	348	16	0	665
	45.26	52.33	2.41	0.00	
	0.91	1.40	0.79	0.00	1.11
Semi-skilled Manual Workers	2,084	609	47	2	2,742
	76.00	22.21	1.71	0.07	
	6.33	2.46	2.33	2.30	4.58
Unskilled Manual Workers	3	3	0	0	6
	50.00	50.00	0.00	0.00	
	0.01	0.01	0.00	0.00	0.01
Unemployed	1,938	745	116	11	2,810
	68.97	26.51	4.13	0.39	
	5.88	3.01	5.76	12.64	4.70
Not Classifiable	1,270	778	60	2	2,110
	60.19	36.87	2.84	0.09	
	3.85	3.14	2.98	2.30	3.53
Home Duties	9,509	6,157	616	18	16,300
	58.34	37.77	3.78	0.11	
	28.86	24.84	30.57	20.69	27.24
Not Stated	366	442	126	6	940
	38.94	47.02	13.40	0.64	
	1.11	1.78	6.25	6.90	1.57
Total	**32,945**	**24,790**	**2,015**	**87**	**59,837**
	55.06	**41.43**	**3.37**	**0.15**	**100.00**

Note:
- 'Not Applicable' is not used in the classification of maternal occupation. See Appendix C for a description of the classification system for occupations.
- 'Not Stated' contains 73 Early Neonatal Deaths for which Type of Feeding was not stated.

Table F17

Infant's Type of Feeding by Maternal Parity, Live Births Only, 2003

Singleton Births

Type of Feeding	Maternal Parity									
Frequency Row Per Cent Col. Per Cent	0	1	2	3	4	5	6	More than 6	Not Stated	Total
Artificial	12,392	10,886	5,875	2,290	860	343	172	126	1	32,945
	37.61	33.04	17.83	6.95	2.61	1.04	0.52	0.38	0.00	
	50.99	57.13	58.01	58.34	58.82	62.94	72.57	70.39	20.00	55.06
Breast	11,013	7,558	3,926	1,481	529	175	57	49	2	24,790
	44.43	30.49	15.84	5.97	2.13	0.71	0.23	0.20	0.01	
	45.32	39.66	38.76	37.73	36.18	32.11	24.05	27.37	40.00	41.43
Combined	854	597	311	148	68	26	8	3	0	2,015
	42.38	29.63	15.43	7.34	3.37	1.29	0.40	0.15	0.00	
	3.51	3.13	3.07	3.77	4.65	4.77	3.38	1.68	0.00	3.37
Not Stated	42	14	16	6	5	1	0	1	2	87
	48.28	16.09	18.39	6.90	5.75	1.15	0.00	1.15	2.30	
	0.17	0.07	0.16	0.15	0.34	0.18	0.00	0.56	40.00	0.15
Total	24,301	19,055	10,128	3,925	1,462	545	237	179	5	59,837
	40.61	31.84	16.93	6.56	2.44	0.91	0.40	0.30	0.01	100.00

Appendix G

Wigglesworth Classification, 2003

Basis of System

In this section perinatal deaths are classified according to the system devised by Dr. J. S. Wigglesworth. The system is purposely designed to be relatively straightforward and to overcome some of the inherent difficulties of subjectivity and lack of uniformity in the assignment of causes of perinatal death.[7] With the aim of identifying areas with implications for perinatal care, five mutually exclusive and clinically relevant categories are suggested. Cross-classification of these categories by birthweight can then be used to highlight areas of particular concern.[8]

Method of Classification

The five broad pathological subgroups employed in the Wigglesworth classification are as follows:

1. Normally formed macerated stillbirth.
2. Congenital malformations (stillbirth or early neonatal death).
3. Conditions associated with immaturity (early neonatal death).
4. Asphyxial conditions developing in labour (stillbirth or early neonatal death).
5. Specific conditions other than the above.

The assignment of a unique Wigglesworth class to each perinatal death presents a number of difficulties. The first and most general of these results from the fact that no standard system has yet been devised for the translation of the ICD codes relating to main cause of death into the corresponding categories suggested by Wigglesworth. In most cases the assignment is straightforward, but in certain instances (for example, preterm births where asphyxia is indicated or stillbirths where antepartum haemorrhage is recorded), the appropriate classification is not immediately obvious and additional variables require consideration. For these reasons, gestational age and type of stillbirth (i.e. antepartum or intrapartum) are taken into account in the classification system described below. In adopting this system, note has also been taken of a number of pilot schemes carried out in Britain as well as the guidelines set out by Dr. Wigglesworth.[9]

---

[7] Wigglesworth, J.S., 1980, "Monitoring Perinatal Mortality", *The Lancet*, Vol. 2, pp.684-686.

[8] The analysis by Wigglesworth's categories, unlike the main report, includes 51 births that weighed less than 500 grams. The outcomes of these births were 31 stillbirths and 20 early neonatal deaths.

[9] a) South East Thames Perinatal Monitoring Group, *Confidential Enquiry into Perinatal Deaths*, 1986.
   b) Unpublished report, "Scottish Stillbirth and Neonatal Death Enquiry", based on 1985 data.

Wiggleworth Classes	Assignment Criteria	ICD Codes (where appropiate)
Macerated stillbirth	• All intrapartum deaths where maceration is indicated as main cause of death. • Antepartum deaths not due to antepartum haemorrhage and not assigned to any other category.	-
Congenital malformations (stillbirth or early neonatal death)	• All major congenital anomalies (stillbirth or early neonatal deaths).	740-742, 745-748, 750.3, 750.6, 751.1-751.8, 753, 756.0, 756.6, 756.7, 758-759
Immaturity (early neonatal death)	• All first week deaths due to structural lung immaturity and Hyaline Membrane Disease. • First week deaths of less than 37 weeks gestation period where cause of death is not stated or does not fall into any other category.	765, 769.0, 770.4, 772.1, 777.5
Asphyxia (stillbirth or early neonatal death)	• All first week deaths due to birth trauma and birth asphyxia. • First week deaths of 37 or more weeks gestation or gestation unknown where cause is not stated or does not fall into any other category. • Antepartum deaths due to antepartum haemorrhage. • All intrapartum stillbirths except those due to specific conditions or congenital malformations.	762.0, 762.1, 762.4, 762.5, 767-768
Specific conditions (stillbirth or early neonatal death)	• Infection, isoimmunisation or other haemorrhage in the newborn.	760.1-760.5, 762.3, 770.0, 771, 773, 775, 777.0, 778.0

Results

Tabulations based on the Wigglesworth classification are presented in the following pages. Table G1 indicates the percentage of perinatal deaths attributable to each cause for 2003. Table G2 provides a classification of cause of death by birthweight and indicates cause and weight specific perinatal mortality rates for 2003. It is this table that shows the practical clinical implications of the Wigglesworth coding. Figure G1 is derived from the data contained in Table G2 and shows how the percentage contribution to perinatal mortality of each cause changes with birthweight group. Table G3 provides the same cross tabulations as Table G2 but uses a different definition of stillbirth based on 28 weeks gestation period. This is provided to facilitate possible local or international comparisons.

Table G1

Wigglesworth Classification for All Perinatal Deaths, 2003

Class	Frequency	Per Cent	Cumulative Frequency	Cumulative Per Cent
Macerated Stillbirths	238	40.68	238	40.68
Congenital Malformations	147	25.13	385	65.81
Immaturity	73	12.48	458	78.29
Asphyxial Conditions	94	16.07	552	94.36
Specific Conditions	33	5.64	585	100.00

Table G2

Birthweight Specific Perinatal Mortality Rates, 2003

Wigglesworth Classification

Birthweight (grams)	Macerated Stillbirths		Congenital Anomalies		Immaturity		Asphyxia		Specific Conditions		Total	
	Number	Rate	Number	Rate	Number	Rate	Number	Rate	Number	Rate	Number	Rate
Under 1000	73	226.71	29	90.06	59	183.23	28	86.96	11	34.16	200	621.12
1000-1499	29	80.56	28	77.78	5	13.89	8	22.22	8	22.22	78	216.67
1500-1999	22	29.37	31	41.39	3	4.01	15	20.03	1	1.34	72	96.13
2000-2499	23	11.68	19	9.65	2	1.02	8	4.06	3	1.52	55	27.93
2500 and over	88	1.50	39	0.67	2	0.03	35	0.60	10	0.17	174	2.97
Not Stated	3	214.29	1	71.43	2	142.86	0	0.00	0	0.00	6	428.57
Total	238	3.84	147	2.37	73	1.18	94	1.52	33	0.53	585	9.43

Table G3

**Numbers of Perinatal Deaths and Mortality Rates
by Cause of Death and Birthweight, 2003**

Wigglesworth Classification
using the ≥28 weeks definition of a Stillbirth

Birthweight (grams)	Macerated Stillbirths		Congenital Anomalies		Immaturity		Asphyxia		Specific Conditions		Total	
	Number	Rate	Number	Rate	Number	Rate	Number	Rate	Number	Rate	Number	Rate
Under 1000	27	110.66	26	106.56	59	241.80	8	32.79	2	8.20	122	500.00
1000-1499	26	74.07	25	71.23	5	14.25	5	14.25	8	22.79	69	196.58
1500-1999	21	28.07	31	41.44	3	4.01	15	20.05	1	1.34	71	94.92
2000-2499	23	11.68	19	9.65	2	1.02	8	4.06	3	1.52	55	27.93
2500 and over	88	1.50	39	0.67	2	0.03	35	0.60	10	0.17	174	2.97
Not Stated	2	153.85	1	76.92	2	153.85	0	0.00	0	0.00	5	384.62
Total	187	3.02	141	2.28	73	1.18	71	1.15	24	0.39	496	8.01

Figure G1

Wigglesworth Classification: Percentage Distribution of Perinatal Cause of Death by Birthweight Groups, 2003

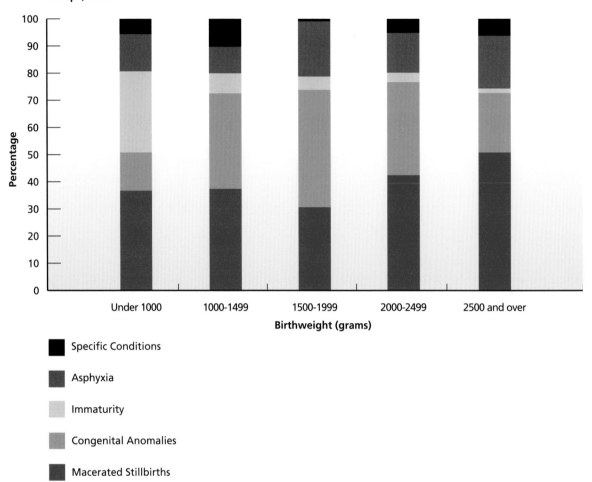

Note: See Appendix G, Table G2 for data. 'Not Stated' data are not included in the calculation of percentages.

Appendix H

Domiciliary Births: 1999-2003
Cross-Tabulations of Selected Variables: 2003

These births have been included, where appropriate, in the analysis presented in previous sections.

In 1999 there were 246 domiciliary births. Of these, there was one early neonatal death and no stillbirths. For 2000 the number of domiciliary births fell to 216 and again reported one early neonatal death and no stillbirths. There were no domiciliary multiple births in 1999 or 2000.

In 2001 the number of domiciliary births increased to 245. Of these, there was one stillbirth and no early neonatal deaths. There was one set of domiciliary twin births in 2001.

The trend in the number of domiciliary births continued to be upwards, increasing to 288 in 2002. Of these, there were no stillbirths and one early neonatal death. There were no domiciliary multiple births in 2002.

In 2003 the number of domiciliary births decreased to 236. Of these, there were no stillbirths and no early neonatal deaths. There were no domiciliary multiple births in 2003.

The tables that follow (H1-H8) present selected statistics on domiciliary births for 1999-2003 and contain a range of cross-tabulations relating to all domiciliary births for 2003. A full list of these tables is given in the Table of Contents. The format of each cross-tabulation is identical. The values of the two variables are given along the top row and left hand side column. The top number in each cell indicates the number of observations relating to that combination of variable values. The second number indicates the percentage contribution of that cell to the total for the whole row. The last number indicates the percentage contribution of that cell to the total for the whole column. The figures at the end of each row or column give the overall total for that row or column, and the associated percentages express each of these figures as a percentage of the grand total.

Table H1

Trends in Selected Statistics, Domiciliary Births, 1999 - 2003

Selected Statistics	1999	2000	2001	2002	2003
General Characteristics					
Average Age of Mother in years	33.47	33.33	33.18	34.07	34.01
Average Maternal Parity	1.52	1.62	1.40	2.07	1.63
Single Mothers (%)	25.20	29.63	31.56	22.57	27.97
Average weight in grams					
- Total Live Births	3699.46	3726.71	3686.75	3730.06	3754.25
Low birthweight <2500 grams (%)					
- Total Live Births	0.43	1.86	0.00	0.35	0.00
Average Gestational Age at delivery in weeks	40.04	39.92	40.02	40.14	40.05
Average interval since last birth in years	3.46	3.40	3.82	3.74	3.65
Perinatal Care					
Midwife and Hospital/GP combined antenatal care (%)*	59.76	57.87	55.33	57.29	66.10
Immunity to Rubella (%)	92.34	90.70	93.44	91.61	94.07
Mother's breastfeeding (%)	98.25	96.63	95.02	94.04	94.07

*This figure applies to the percentage of homebirths where Antenatal Care is stated as 'Combined', rather than Antenatal Care with 'Midwife Only'.

Note:
- There were no domiciliary multiple births in either 1999 or 2000.
- There was 1 set of domiciliary Twin births in 2001.
- There were no domiciliary multiple births in 2002 or 2003.
- Missing values are not included in the calculation of percentages.

Table H2

Age of Mother by Maternal Parity, 2003

Domiciliary Births

Age of Mother	Maternal Parity						
Frequency Row Per Cent Col. Per Cent	0	1	2	3	4	5	Total
15-19 Years	2	0	0	0	0	0	2
	100.00	0.00	0.00	0.00	0.00	0.00	
	5.71	0.00	0.00	0.00	0.00	0.00	0.85
20-24 Years	4	3	0	0	0	0	7
	57.14	42.86	0.00	0.00	0.00	0.00	
	11.43	3.53	0.00	0.00	0.00	0.00	2.97
25-29 Years	11	19	9	2	1	0	42
	26.19	45.24	21.43	4.76	2.38	0.00	
	31.43	22.35	13.04	6.67	7.69	0.00	17.80
30-34 Years	13	36	17	5	2	2	75
	17.33	48.00	22.67	6.67	2.67	2.67	
	37.14	42.35	24.64	16.67	15.38	50.00	31.78
35-39 Years	5	18	34	17	7	2	83
	6.02	21.69	40.96	20.48	8.43	2.41	
	14.29	21.18	49.28	56.67	53.85	50.00	35.17
40-44 Years	0	8	9	5	3	0	25
	0.00	32.00	36.00	20.00	12.00	0.00	
	0.00	9.41	13.04	16.67	23.08	0.00	10.59
45 Years and over	0	0	0	1	0	0	1
	0.00	0.00	0.00	100.00	0.00	0.00	
	0.00	0.00	0.00	3.33	0.00	0.00	0.42
Not Stated	0	1	0	0	0	0	1
	0.00	100.00	0.00	0.00	0.00	0.00	
	0.00	1.18	0.00	0.00	0.00	0.00	0.42
Total	35	85	69	30	13	4	236
	14.83	36.02	29.24	12.71	5.51	1.69	100.00

Table H3

Age of Mother by Gestation Period at Delivery, 2003

Domiciliary Births

Age of Mother	Gestation Period (weeks)			
Frequency Row Per Cent Col. Per Cent	32-36	37-41	42 and over	Total
15-19 Years	0 0.00 0.00	1 50.00 0.47	1 50.00 5.00	2 0.85
20-24 Years	0 0.00 0.00	6 85.71 2.79	1 14.29 5.00	7 2.97
25-29 Years	1 2.38 100.00	40 95.24 18.60	1 2.38 5.00	42 17.80
30-34 Years	0 0.00 0.00	65 86.67 30.23	10 13.33 50.00	75 31.78
35-39 Years	0 0.00 0.00	78 93.98 36.28	5 6.02 25.00	83 35.17
40-44 Years	0 0.00 0.00	24 96.00 11.16	1 4.00 5.00	25 10.59
45 Years and over	0 0.00 0.00	1 100.00 0.47	0 0.00 0.00	1 0.42
Not Stated	0 0.00 0.00	0 0.00 0.00	1 100.00 5.00	1 0.42
Total	1 0.42	215 91.10	20 8.47	236 100.00

Table H4

Birthweight by Gestation Period at Delivery, 2003

Domiciliary Births

Birthweight (grams)	Gestation Period (weeks)			
Frequency Row Per Cent Col. Per Cent	32-36	37-41	42 and over	Total
2500-2999	0	9	0	9
	0.00	100.00	0.00	
	0.00	4.19	0.00	3.81
3000-3499	0	52	4	56
	0.00	92.86	7.14	
	0.00	24.19	20.00	23.73
3500-3999	1	92	8	101
	0.99	91.09	7.92	
	100.00	42.79	40.00	42.80
4000-4499	0	44	6	50
	0.00	88.00	12.00	
	0.00	20.47	30.00	21.19
4500 and over	0	18	2	20
	0.00	90.00	10.00	
	0.00	8.37	10.00	8.47
Total	1	215	20	236
	0.42	91.10	8.47	100.00

Table H5

Mother's Occupation by Birthweight, 2003

Domiciliary Births

Mother's Occupation	Birthweight (grams)					
Frequency Row Per Cent Col. Per Cent	2500-2999	3000-3499	3500-3999	4000-4499	4500 and over	Total
Farmers & Farm	1	0	0	0	0	1
Managers	100.00	0.00	0.00	0.00	0.00	
	11.11	0.00	0.00	0.00	0.00	0.42
Other Agricultural	0	1	0	1	0	2
Occupations &	0.00	50.00	0.00	50.00	0.00	
Fishermen	0.00	1.79	0.00	2.00	0.00	0.85
Higher-Professional	0	3	10	7	2	22
	0.00	13.64	45.45	31.82	9.09	
	0.00	5.36	9.90	14.00	10.00	9.32
Lower-Professional	3	16	31	19	4	73
	4.11	21.92	42.47	26.03	5.48	
	33.33	28.57	30.69	38.00	20.00	30.93
Managers	0	2	3	1	0	6
	0.00	33.33	50.00	16.67	0.00	
	0.00	3.57	2.97	2.00	0.00	2.54
Salaried-Employees	0	1	0	0	1	2
	0.00	50.00	0.00	0.00	50.00	
	0.00	1.79	0.00	0.00	5.00	0.85
Non-Manual	0	4	11	5	2	22
Workers	0.00	18.18	50.00	22.73	9.09	
	0.00	7.14	10.89	10.00	10.00	9.32
Other Non-Manual	0	4	7	3	2	16
Workers	0.00	25.00	43.75	18.75	12.50	
	0.00	7.14	6.93	6.00	10.00	6.78
Skilled Manual	0	3	2	1	0	6
Workers	0.00	50.00	33.33	16.67	0.00	
	0.00	5.36	1.98	2.00	0.00	2.54
Unemployed	0	4	2	0	0	6
	0.00	66.67	33.33	0.00	0.00	
	0.00	7.14	1.98	0.00	0.00	2.54
Not Classifiable	0	1	4	1	0	6
	0.00	16.67	66.67	16.67	0.00	
	0.00	1.79	3.96	2.00	0.00	2.54
Home Duties	5	17	29	11	8	70
	7.14	24.29	41.43	15.71	11.43	
	55.56	30.36	28.71	22.00	40.00	29.66
Not Stated	0	0	2	1	1	4
	0.00	0.00	50.00	25.00	25.00	
	0.00	0.00	1.98	2.00	5.00	1.69
Total	**9**	**56**	**101**	**50**	**20**	**236**
	3.81	**23.73**	**42.80**	**21.19**	**8.47**	**100.00**

Note: 'Not Applicable' is not used in the classification of maternal occupation. See Appendix C for a description of the classification system for occupations.

Table H6

Marital Status by Age of Mother, 2003

Domiciliary Births

Marital Status	Age of Mother (Years)								
Frequency Row Per Cent Col. Per Cent	15-19	20-24	25-29	30-34	35-39	40-44	45 and over	Not Stated	Total
Married	0	2	24	54	65	17	1	1	164
	0.00	1.22	14.63	32.93	39.63	10.37	0.61	0.61	
	0.00	28.57	57.14	72.00	78.31	68.00	100.00	100.00	69.49
Single	2	5	16	21	15	7	0	0	66
	3.03	7.58	24.24	31.82	22.73	10.61	0.00	0.00	
	100.00	71.43	38.10	28.00	18.07	28.00	0.00	0.00	27.97
Widowed	0	0	1	0	0	0	0	0	1
	0.00	0.00	100.00	0.00	0.00	0.00	0.00	0.00	
	0.00	0.00	2.38	0.00	0.00	0.00	0.00	0.00	0.42
Separated	0	0	1	0	1	0	0	0	2
	0.00	0.00	50.00	0.00	50.00	0.00	0.00	0.00	
	0.00	0.00	2.38	0.00	1.20	0.00	0.00	0.00	0.85
Divorced	0	0	0	0	2	1	0	0	3
	0.00	0.00	0.00	0.00	66.67	33.33	0.00	0.00	
	0.00	0.00	0.00	0.00	2.41	4.00	0.00	0.00	1.27
Total	2	7	42	75	83	25	1	1	236
	0.85	2.97	17.80	31.78	35.17	10.59	0.42	0.42	100.00

Table H7

Father's Occupation by Infant's Type of Feeding, Live Births Only, 2003

Domiciliary Births

Father's Occupation	Type of Feeding			
Frequency Row Per Cent Col. Per Cent	Artificial	Breast	Combined	Total
Farmers & Farm Managers	0 0.00 0.00	7 100.00 3.15	0 0.00 0.00	7 2.97
Other Agricultural Occupations & Fishermen	0 0.00 0.00	6 100.00 2.70	0 0.00 0.00	6 2.54
Higher-Professional	1 3.03 10.00	32 96.97 14.41	0 0.00 0.00	33 13.98
Lower-Professional	1 2.17 10.00	45 97.83 20.27	0 0.00 0.00	46 19.49
Managers	1 5.00 10.00	19 95.00 8.56	0 0.00 0.00	20 8.47
Salaried-Employees	1 11.11 10.00	8 88.89 3.60	0 0.00 0.00	9 3.81
Non-Manual Workers	0 0.00 0.00	13 100.00 5.86	0 0.00 0.00	13 5.51
Other Non-Manual Workers	2 10.53 20.00	16 84.21 7.21	1 5.26 25.00	19 8.05
Skilled Manual Workers	3 4.62 30.00	59 90.77 26.58	3 4.62 75.00	65 27.54
Semi-skilled Manual Workers	1 14.29 10.00	6 85.71 2.70	0 0.00 0.00	7 2.97
Unskilled Manual Workers	0 0.00 0.00	1 100.00 0.45	0 0.00 0.00	1 0.42
Not Classifiable	0 0.00 0.00	4 100.00 1.80	0 0.00 0.00	4 1.69
Not Applicable	0 0.00 0.00	3 100.00 1.35	0 0.00 0.00	3 1.27
Not Stated	0 0.00 0.00	3 100.00 1.35	0 0.00 0.00	3 1.27
Total	10 4.24	222 94.07	4 1.69	236 100.00

Note: In this table 'Not Classifiable' includes 1 father whose occupation was recorded as 'Home Duties'.

Table H8

Mother's Occupation by Infant's Type of Feeding, Live Births Only, 2003

Domiciliary Births

Mother's Occupation	Type of Feeding			
Frequency **Row Per Cent** **Col. Per Cent**	**Artificial**	**Breast**	**Combined**	**Total**
Farmers & Farm Managers	0 0.00 0.00	1 100.00 0.45	0 0.00 0.00	1 0.42
Other Agricultural Occupations & Fishermen	0 0.00 0.00	2 100.00 0.90	0 0.00 0.00	2 0.85
Higher-Professional	1 4.55 10.00	21 95.45 9.46	0 0.00 0.00	22 9.32
Lower-Professional	3 4.11 30.00	70 95.89 31.53	0 0.00 0.00	73 30.93
Managers	0 0.00 0.00	6 100.00 2.70	0 0.00 0.00	6 2.54
Salaried-Employees	0 0.00 0.00	2 100.00 0.90	0 0.00 0.00	2 0.85
Non-Manual Workers	2 9.09 20.00	20 90.91 9.01	0 0.00 0.00	22 9.32
Other Non-Manual Workers	2 12.50 20.00	14 87.50 6.31	0 0.00 0.00	16 6.78
Skilled Manual Workers	0 0.00 0.00	5 83.33 2.25	1 16.67 25.00	6 2.54
Unemployed	0 0.00 0.00	6 100.00 2.70	0 0.00 0.00	6 2.54
Not Classifiable	1 16.67 10.00	5 83.33 2.25	0 0.00 0.00	6 2.54
Home Duties	1 1.43 10.00	66 94.29 29.73	3 4.29 75.00	70 29.66
Not Stated	0 0.00 0.00	4 100.00 1.80	0 0.00 0.00	4 1.69
Total	**10** **4.24**	**222** **94.07**	**4** **1.69**	**236** **100.00**

Note: 'Not Applicable' is not used in the classification of maternal occupation. See Appendix C for a description of the classification system for occupations.

Appendix I

Gestational Age at Time of First Visit to Doctor or Hospital During Pregnancy

Participation in a European Project (Euro-Peristat II Project) resulted in a review in 2006 of the formula used in the analysis of these data. To be consistent with the European standard for this variable, the following formula is being applied to this calculation:

$$\text{GestVis} = \text{HospDoc} - (\text{InfDOB} - (\text{Gestat} \times 7))$$

GestVis = gestational age at date of the first visit to doctor or hospital during pregnancy.
HospDoc = first antenatal visit date (either doctor or hospital).
InfDOB = infant's date of birth.
Gestat*7 = gestation at delivery in days.
The initial calculation produces a period measured in days, which is then converted into weeks for reporting.

To facilitate trend analysis for this variable, data for the period 1999 to 2003 are presented here (and have been estimated using the formula presented above).

The format of each cross-tabulation are identical. The values of the two variables are given along the top row and left hand side column. The top number in each cell indicates the number of observations relating to that combination of variable values. The second number indicates the percentage contribution of that cell to the total for the whole row. The last number indicates the percentage contribution of that cell to the total for the whole column. The figures at the end of each row or column give the overall total for that row or column, and the associated percentages express each of these figures as a percentage of the grand total.

Table I1

Time of First Visit to Doctor or Hospital During Pregnancy

Live Births, Stillbirths, Early Neonatal Deaths
and Mortality Rates, 1999-2003

Singleton Births

1999

Time of First Visit (Weeks)	Live Births	Per Cent (%) Live Births	Stillbirths	Stillbirth Rate	Early Neonatal Deaths	Early Neonatal Rate	Perinatal Mortality Rate	Adjusted PMR
0-12	25,592	48.7	127	4.9	57	2.2	7.2	5.3
13-19	15,904	30.3	74	4.6	33	2.1	6.7	4.7
20 and over	8,035	15.3	49	6.1	28	3.5	9.5	7.1
Not Stated	3,025	5.8	24	7.9	12	4.0	11.8	10.8
Total	52,556	100.0	274	5.2	130	2.5	7.6	5.7

2000

Time of First Visit (Weeks)	Live Births	Per Cent (%) Live Births	Stillbirths	Stillbirth Rate	Early Neonatal Deaths	Early Neonatal Rate	Perinatal Mortality Rate	Adjusted PMR
0-12	26,630	49.8	131	4.9	60	2.3	7.1	5.1
13-19	16,000	29.9	87	5.4	43	2.7	8.1	5.7
20 and over	8,262	15.5	52	6.3	37	4.5	10.7	7.8
Not Stated	2,550	4.8	25	9.7	13	5.1	14.8	12.8
Total	53,442	100.0	295	5.5	153	2.9	8.3	6.0

2001

Time of First Visit (Weeks)	Live Births	Per Cent (%) Live Births	Stillbirths	Stillbirth Rate	Early Neonatal Deaths	Early Neonatal Rate	Perinatal Mortality Rate	Adjusted PMR
0-12	26,001	46.3	122	4.7	57	2.2	6.9	4.7
13-19	16,279	29.0	102	6.2	38	2.3	8.5	5.9
20 and over	10,125	18.0	55	5.4	26	2.6	8.0	5.7
Not Stated	3,710	6.6	28	7.5	15	4.0	11.5	9.1
Total	56,115	100.0	307	5.4	136	2.4	7.9	5.5

2002

Time of First Visit (Weeks)	Live Births	Per Cent (%) Live Births	Stillbirths	Stillbirth Rate	Early Neonatal Deaths	Early Neonatal Rate	Perinatal Mortality Rate	Adjusted PMR
0-12	26,761	45.5	127	4.7	52	1.9	6.7	4.8
13-19	17,999	30.6	100	5.5	44	2.4	8.0	5.7
20 and over	10,526	17.9	71	6.7	39	3.7	10.4	8.6
Not Stated	3,466	5.9	21	6.0	14	4.0	10.0	8.6
Total	58,752	100.0	319	5.4	149	2.5	7.9	6.0

2003

Time of First Visit (Weeks)	Live Births	Per Cent (%) Live Births	Stillbirths	Stillbirth Rate	Early Neonatal Deaths	Early Neonatal Rate	Perinatal Mortality Rate	Adjusted PMR
0-12	26,923	45.0	128	4.7	55	2.0	6.8	4.6
13-19	20,069	33.5	108	5.4	51	2.5	7.9	5.4
20 and over	9,860	16.5	67	6.7	39	4.0	10.7	7.7
Not Stated	2,985	5.0	24	8.0	11	3.7	11.6	9.0
Total	59,837	100.0	327	5.4	156	2.6	8.0	5.6

Table I2

Time of First Visit to Doctor or Hospital During Pregnancy

Live Births, Stillbirths, Early Neonatal Deaths
and Mortality Rates, 1999-2003

Multiple Births

1999

Time of First Visit (Weeks)	Live Births	Per Cent (%) Live Births	Stillbirths	Stillbirth Rate	Early Neonatal Deaths	Early Neonatal Rate	Perinatal Mortality Rate	Adjusted PMR
0-12	770	52.6	6	7.7	9	11.7	19.3	18.1
13-19	385	26.3	4	10.3	7	18.2	28.3	28.3
20 and over	200	13.7	4	19.6	8	40.0	58.8	44.8
Not Stated	108	7.4	0	0.0	3	27.8	27.8	27.8
Total	1,463	100.0	14	9.5	27	18.5	27.8	25.1

2000

Time of First Visit (Weeks)	Live Births	Per Cent (%) Live Births	Stillbirths	Stillbirth Rate	Early Neonatal Deaths	Early Neonatal Rate	Perinatal Mortality Rate	Adjusted PMR
0-12	698	48.8	6	8.5	9	12.9	21.3	14.3
13-19	382	26.7	4	10.4	4	10.5	20.7	10.5
20 and over	224	15.7	8	34.5	6	26.8	60.3	48.0
Not Stated	125	8.7	2	15.7	4	32.0	47.2	47.2
Total	1,429	100.0	20	13.8	23	16.1	29.7	21.6

2001

Time of First Visit (Weeks)	Live Births	Per Cent (%) Live Births	Stillbirths	Stillbirth Rate	Early Neonatal Deaths	Early Neonatal Rate	Perinatal Mortality Rate	Adjusted PMR
0-12	860	47.6	19	21.6	7	8.1	29.6	25.1
13-19	511	28.3	5	9.7	8	15.7	25.2	17.6
20 and over	303	16.8	8	25.7	8	26.4	51.4	42.2
Not Stated	133	7.4	0	0.0	1	7.5	7.5	7.5
Total	1,807	100.0	32	17.4	24	13.3	30.5	24.6

2002

Time of First Visit (Weeks)	Live Births	Per Cent (%) Live Births	Stillbirths	Stillbirth Rate	Early Neonatal Deaths	Early Neonatal Rate	Perinatal Mortality Rate	Adjusted PMR
0-12	820	46.3	8	9.7	10	12.2	21.7	21.7
13-19	521	29.4	9	17.0	6	11.5	28.3	24.6
20 and over	297	16.8	6	19.8	5	16.8	36.3	36.3
Not Stated	132	7.5	1	7.5	0	0.0	7.5	7.5
Total	1,770	100.0	24	13.4	21	11.9	25.1	24.0

2003

Time of First Visit (Weeks)	Live Births	Per Cent (%) Live Births	Stillbirths	Stillbirth Rate	Early Neonatal Deaths	Early Neonatal Rate	Perinatal Mortality Rate	Adjusted PMR
0-12	897	50.0	12	13.2	10	11.1	24.2	22.1
13-19	568	31.6	14	24.1	6	10.6	34.4	34.4
20 and over	211	11.8	1	4.7	1	4.7	9.4	9.4
Not Stated	119	6.6	3	24.6	4	33.6	57.4	49.6
Total	1,795	100.0	30	16.4	21	11.7	27.9	26.3

Table I3

**Marital Status by Gestational Age at Time of First Visit to Doctor or Hospital During Pregnancy,
Live Births and Stillbirths, 1999-2003**

Singleton Births

1999

Marital Status	Gestational Age at First Visit (weeks)				
Frequency Row Per Cent Col. Per Cent	0-12	13-19	20 and over	Not Stated	Total
Married	18,625	10,447	4,527	2,469	36,068
	51.64	28.96	12.55	6.85	
	72.42	65.38	56.00	80.98	68.27
Single	6,644	5,232	3,360	513	15,749
	42.19	33.22	21.33	3.26	
	25.83	32.75	41.56	16.83	29.81
Widowed	33	20	13	3	69
	47.83	28.99	18.84	4.35	
	0.13	0.13	0.16	0.10	0.13
Separated	364	248	164	27	803
	45.33	30.88	20.42	3.36	
	1.42	1.55	2.03	0.89	1.52
Divorced	47	25	17	2	91
	51.65	27.47	18.68	2.20	
	0.18	0.16	0.21	0.07	0.17
Not Stated	6	6	3	35	50
	12.00	12.00	6.00	70.00	
	0.02	0.04	0.04	1.15	0.09
Total	25,719	15,978	8,084	3,049	52,830
	48.68	30.24	15.30	5.77	100.00

2000

Marital Status	Gestational Age at First Visit (weeks)				
Frequency Row Per Cent Col. Per Cent	0-12	13-19	20 and over	Not Stated	Total
Married	19,232	10,351	4,762	2,108	36,453
	52.76	28.40	13.06	5.78	
	71.87	64.34	57.28	81.86	67.84
Single	7,067	5,409	3,328	430	16,234
	43.53	33.32	20.50	2.65	
	26.41	33.62	40.03	16.70	30.21
Widowed	32	19	18	3	72
	44.44	26.39	25.00	4.17	
	0.12	0.12	0.22	0.12	0.13
Separated	357	270	174	23	824
	43.33	32.77	21.12	2.79	
	1.33	1.68	2.09	0.89	1.53
Divorced	73	38	29	7	147
	49.66	25.85	19.73	4.76	
	0.27	0.24	0.35	0.27	0.27
Not Stated	0	0	3	4	7
	0.00	0.00	42.86	57.14	
	0.00	0.00	0.04	0.16	0.01
Total	26,761	16,087	8,314	2,575	53,737
	49.80	29.94	15.47	4.79	100.00

Table I3 Continued
Marital Status by Gestational Age at Time of First Visit to Doctor or Hospital During Pregnancy,
Live Births and Stillbirths, 1999-2003
Singleton Births

2001

Marital Status	Gestational Age at First Visit (weeks)				
Frequency Row Per Cent Col. Per Cent	0-12	13-19	20 and over	Not Stated	Total
Married	18,800	10,477	5,944	3,187	38,408
	48.95	27.28	15.48	8.30	
	71.97	63.96	58.39	85.26	68.07
Single	6,927	5,607	4,032	515	17,081
	40.55	32.83	23.61	3.02	
	26.52	34.23	39.61	13.78	30.27
Widowed	33	20	24	5	82
	40.24	24.39	29.27	6.10	
	0.13	0.12	0.24	0.13	0.15
Separated	306	230	150	25	711
	43.04	32.35	21.10	3.52	
	1.17	1.40	1.47	0.67	1.26
Divorced	57	47	29	3	136
	41.91	34.56	21.32	2.21	
	0.22	0.29	0.28	0.08	0.24
Not Stated	0	0	1	3	4
	0.00	0.00	25.00	75.00	
	0.00	0.00	0.01	0.08	0.01
Total	26,123	16,381	10,180	3,738	56,422
	46.30	29.03	18.04	6.63	100.00

2002

Marital Status	Gestational Age at First Visit (weeks)				
Frequency Row Per Cent Col. Per Cent	0-12	13-19	20 and over	Not Stated	Total
Married	19,239	11,540	6,444	3,086	40,309
	47.73	28.63	15.99	7.66	
	71.55	63.76	60.81	88.50	68.24
Single	7,249	6,231	3,946	379	17,805
	40.71	35.00	22.16	2.13	
	26.96	34.43	37.24	10.87	30.14
Widowed	30	28	20	1	79
	37.97	35.44	25.32	1.27	
	0.11	0.15	0.19	0.03	0.13
Separated	299	245	151	14	709
	42.17	34.56	21.30	1.97	
	1.11	1.35	1.42	0.40	1.20
Divorced	71	54	32	5	162
	43.83	33.33	19.75	3.09	
	0.26	0.30	0.30	0.14	0.27
Not Stated	0	1	4	2	7
	0.00	14.29	57.14	28.57	
	0.00	0.01	0.04	0.06	0.01
Total	26,888	18,099	10,597	3,487	59,071
	45.52	30.64	17.94	5.90	100.00

Table I3 Continued

Marital Status by Gestational Age at Time of First Visit to Doctor or Hospital During Pregnancy, Live Births and Stillbirths, 1999-2003

Singleton Births

2003

Marital Status Frequency Row Per Cent Col. Per Cent	Gestational Age at First Visit (weeks)				
	0-12	13-19	20 and over	Not Stated	Total
Married	19,584	12,868	5,916	2,621	40,989
	47.78	31.39	14.43	6.39	
	72.40	63.78	59.60	87.11	68.13
Single	7,105	6,990	3,784	360	18,239
	38.95	38.32	20.75	1.97	
	26.27	34.64	38.12	11.96	30.32
Widowed	30	12	18	1	61
	49.18	19.67	29.51	1.64	
	0.11	0.06	0.18	0.03	0.10
Separated	242	239	170	20	671
	36.07	35.62	25.34	2.98	
	0.89	1.18	1.71	0.66	1.12
Divorced	89	68	36	5	198
	44.95	34.34	18.18	2.53	
	0.33	0.34	0.36	0.17	0.33
Not Stated	1	0	3	2	6
	16.67	0.00	50.00	33.33	
	0.00	0.00	0.03	0.07	0.01
Total	27,051	20,177	9,927	3,009	60,164
	44.96	33.54	16.50	5.00	100.00

Table I4

Interval in Years Since Last Birth by Gestational Age at Time of First Visit to Doctor or Hospital During Pregnancy, Live Births and Stillbirths, 1999-2003
Singleton Births

1999

Interval Since Last Birth — Frequency / Row Per Cent / Col. Per Cent	Gestational Age at First Visit (weeks)				
	0-12	13-19	20 and over	Not Stated	Total
No Previous Births	11,178	6,378	3,002	1,120	21,678
	51.56	29.42	13.85	5.17	
	43.46	39.92	37.14	36.73	41.03
1 year or less	170	114	158	56	498
	34.14	22.89	31.73	11.24	
	0.66	0.71	1.95	1.84	0.94
>1 year to 2 years	2,990	2,278	1,485	486	7,239
	41.30	31.47	20.51	6.71	
	11.63	14.26	18.37	15.94	13.70
>2 years to 3 years	3,762	2,483	1,159	492	7,896
	47.64	31.45	14.68	6.23	
	14.63	15.54	14.34	16.14	14.95
>3 years to 4 years	2,520	1,534	760	268	5,082
	49.59	30.18	14.95	5.27	
	9.80	9.60	9.40	8.79	9.62
>4 years to 5 years	1,548	983	410	169	3,110
	49.77	31.61	13.18	5.43	
	6.02	6.15	5.07	5.54	5.89
>5 years to 6 years	976	611	296	93	1,976
	49.39	30.92	14.98	4.71	
	3.79	3.82	3.66	3.05	3.74
More than 6 years	2,425	1,490	687	227	4,829
	50.22	30.86	14.23	4.70	
	9.43	9.33	8.50	7.45	9.14
Number of Previous Births Unknown	1	3	0	14	18
	5.56	16.67	0.00	77.78	
	0.00	0.02	0.00	0.46	0.03
Not Stated	149	104	127	124	504
	29.56	20.63	25.20	24.60	
	0.58	0.65	1.57	4.07	0.95
Total	25,719	15,978	8,084	3,049	52,830
	48.68	30.24	15.30	5.77	100.00

Table I4 Continued
Interval in Years Since Last Birth by Gestational Age at Time of First Visit to Doctor or Hospital During Pregnancy, Live Births and Stillbirths, 1999-2003
Singleton Births

2000

Interval Since Last Birth	Gestational Age at First Visit (weeks)				
Frequency Row Per Cent Col. Per Cent	0-12	13-19	20 and over	Not Stated	Total
No Previous Births	11,437	6,404	3,175	1,010	22,026
	51.92	29.07	14.41	4.59	
	42.74	39.81	38.19	39.22	40.99
1 year or less	171	128	145	31	475
	36.00	26.95	30.53	6.53	
	0.64	0.80	1.74	1.20	0.88
>1 year to 2 years	3,239	2,252	1,414	404	7,309
	44.32	30.81	19.35	5.53	
	12.10	14.00	17.01	15.69	13.60
>2 years to 3 years	4,058	2,440	1,198	408	8,104
	50.07	30.11	14.78	5.03	
	15.16	15.17	14.41	15.84	15.08
>3 years to 4 years	2,699	1,626	744	239	5,308
	50.85	30.63	14.02	4.50	
	10.09	10.11	8.95	9.28	9.88
>4 years to 5 years	1,582	977	463	128	3,150
	50.22	31.02	14.70	4.06	
	5.91	6.07	5.57	4.97	5.86
>5 years to 6 years	1,016	637	301	82	2,036
	49.90	31.29	14.78	4.03	
	3.80	3.96	3.62	3.18	3.79
More than 6 years	2,435	1,522	773	185	4,915
	49.54	30.97	15.73	3.76	
	9.10	9.46	9.30	7.18	9.15
Not Stated	124	101	101	88	414
	29.95	24.40	24.40	21.26	
	0.46	0.63	1.21	3.42	0.77
Total	26,761	16,087	8,314	2,575	53,737
	49.80	29.94	15.47	4.79	100.00

Table I4 Continued
Interval in Years Since Last Birth by Gestational Age at Time of First Visit to Doctor or Hospital During Pregnancy, Live Births and Stillbirths, 1999-2003
Singleton Births

2001

Interval Since Last Birth	Gestational Age at First Visit (weeks)				
Frequency Row Per Cent Col. Per Cent	0-12	13-19	20 and over	Not Stated	Total
No Previous Births	11,148	6,476	4,137	1,436	23,197
	48.06	27.92	17.83	6.19	
	42.68	39.53	40.64	38.42	41.11
1 year or less	181	159	203	33	576
	31.42	27.60	35.24	5.73	
	0.69	0.97	1.99	0.88	1.02
>1 year to 2 years	3,093	2,203	1,585	609	7,490
	41.30	29.41	21.16	8.13	
	11.84	13.45	15.57	16.29	13.27
>2 years to 3 years	3,926	2,506	1,400	600	8,432
	46.56	29.72	16.60	7.12	
	15.03	15.30	13.75	16.05	14.94
>3 years to 4 years	2,685	1,661	827	357	5,530
	48.55	30.04	14.95	6.46	
	10.28	10.14	8.12	9.55	9.80
>4 years to 5 years	1,689	1,075	554	201	3,519
	48.00	30.55	15.74	5.71	
	6.47	6.56	5.44	5.38	6.24
>5 years to 6 years	998	661	393	117	2,169
	46.01	30.47	18.12	5.39	
	3.82	4.04	3.86	3.13	3.84
More than 6 years	2,286	1,536	929	237	4,988
	45.83	30.79	18.62	4.75	
	8.75	9.38	9.13	6.34	8.84
Number of Previous Births Unknown	4	2	4	4	14
	28.57	14.29	28.57	28.57	
	0.02	0.01	0.04	0.11	0.02
Not Stated	113	102	148	144	507
	22.29	20.12	29.19	28.40	
	0.43	0.62	1.45	3.85	0.90
Total	26,123	16,381	10,180	3,738	56,422
	46.30	29.03	18.04	6.63	100.00

Table I4 Continued
Interval in Years Since Last Birth by Gestational Age at Time of First Visit to Doctor or Hospital During Pregnancy, Live Births and Stillbirths, 1999-2003
Singleton Births

2002

Interval Since Last Birth	Gestational Age at First Visit (weeks)				
Frequency Row Per Cent Col. Per Cent	0-12	13-19	20 and over	Not Stated	Total
No Previous Births	11,392	7,212	4,194	1,359	24,157
	47.16	29.85	17.36	5.63	
	42.37	39.85	39.58	38.97	40.89
1 year or less	166	144	172	38	520
	31.92	27.69	33.08	7.31	
	0.62	0.80	1.62	1.09	0.88
>1 year to 2 years	3,214	2,469	1,833	509	8,025
	40.05	30.77	22.84	6.34	
	11.95	13.64	17.30	14.60	13.59
>2 years to 3 years	4,004	2,731	1,360	562	8,657
	46.25	31.55	15.71	6.49	
	14.89	15.09	12.83	16.12	14.66
>3 years to 4 years	2,708	1,772	833	330	5,643
	47.99	31.40	14.76	5.85	
	10.07	9.79	7.86	9.46	9.55
>4 years to 5 years	1,758	1,148	616	200	3,722
	47.23	30.84	16.55	5.37	
	6.54	6.34	5.81	5.74	6.30
>5 years to 6 years	1,060	791	418	103	2,372
	44.69	33.35	17.62	4.34	
	3.94	4.37	3.94	2.95	4.02
More than 6 years	2,452	1,716	1,025	209	5,402
	45.39	31.77	18.97	3.87	
	9.12	9.48	9.67	5.99	9.14
Number of Previous Births Unknown	0	0	0	2	2
	0.00	0.00	0.00	100.00	
	0.00	0.00	0.00	0.06	0.00
Not Stated	134	116	146	175	571
	23.47	20.32	25.57	30.65	
	0.50	0.64	1.38	5.02	0.97
Total	26,888	18,099	10,597	3,487	59,071
	45.52	30.64	17.94	5.90	100.00

Table I4 Continued

Interval in Years Since Last Birth by Gestational Age at Time of First Visit to Doctor or Hospital During Pregnancy, Live Births and Stillbirths, 1999-2003

Singleton Births

2003

Interval Since Last Birth	Gestational Age at First Visit (weeks)				
Frequency **Row Per Cent** **Col. Per Cent**	**0-12**	**13-19**	**20 and over**	**Not Stated**	**Total**
No Previous Births	11,308	8,062	3,937	1,149	24,456
	46.24	32.97	16.10	4.70	
	41.80	39.96	39.66	38.19	40.65
1 year or less	180	183	181	18	562
	32.03	32.56	32.21	3.20	
	0.67	0.91	1.82	0.60	0.93
>1 year to 2 years	3,593	2,899	1,755	430	8,677
	41.41	33.41	20.23	4.96	
	13.28	14.37	17.68	14.29	14.42
>2 years to 3 years	4,066	3,041	1,382	483	8,972
	45.32	33.89	15.40	5.38	
	15.03	15.07	13.92	16.05	14.91
>3 years to 4 years	2,687	1,922	805	267	5,681
	47.30	33.83	14.17	4.70	
	9.93	9.53	8.11	8.87	9.44
>4 years to 5 years	1,704	1,226	487	153	3,570
	47.73	34.34	13.64	4.29	
	6.30	6.08	4.91	5.08	5.93
>5 years to 6 years	1,094	808	324	102	2,328
	46.99	34.71	13.92	4.38	
	4.04	4.00	3.26	3.39	3.87
More than 6 years	2,305	1,909	914	172	5,300
	43.49	36.02	17.25	3.25	
	8.52	9.46	9.21	5.72	8.81
Number of Previous Births Unknown	0	0	0	2	2
	0.00	0.00	0.00	100.00	
	0.00	0.00	0.00	0.07	0.00
Not Stated	114	127	142	233	616
	18.51	20.62	23.05	37.82	
	0.42	0.63	1.43	7.74	1.02
Total	**27,051**	**20,177**	**9,927**	**3,009**	**60,164**
	44.96	**33.54**	**16.50**	**5.00**	**100.00**